KYLIE Minogue

the superstar next door

BY SASHA STONE

Omnibus Press

London   New York   Sydney

M B I
MEDIA BUSINESS INTERNATIONAL

Exclusive distributors:

BOOK SALES LIMITED,
8/9 Frith Street,
London W1V 5TZ, UK.

MUSIC SALES CORPORATION,
225 Park Avenue South,
New York, NY 10003, USA.

MUSIC SALES PTY LIMITED,
120 Rothschild Avenue,
Rosebery, NSW 2018, Australia.

To the Music Trade only:
MUSIC SALES LIMITED,
8/9 Frith Street,
London W1V 5TZ, UK.

PICTURE CREDITS:
Alpha Photographs: p5, 6, 21, 30/1, 33(L),
33(R), 53(T), 60(T), 66(B), 70(CL), 70(CR),
73(R), 85, 86/7, 87.
Tim Anderson: p19.
Hutchison Picture Agency: p89.
Pictorial Press: p9, 93.
Press Association: p15(T), 16, 17, 54/5, 68, 84.
Profile Press: p16, 17, 59, 61, 62, 63(TR),
65, 70(TC).
Rex Features: Front Cover, 3, 4, 7, 8(L), 8/9,
10, 10/11, 11, 13, 23, 24, 25, 26, 27, 29, 32,
33(L), 33(R), 34, 35(L), 35(R), 36, 37, 39,
49, 50, 51, 57(L), 57(R), 58, 60, 63(TL),
63(R), 64, 67, 69, 70(CR), 71, 72, 73(L), 88,
91, 93, 94, 95, 96.
Scan Press: p52, 53(B), 56, 70(T), 74, 75,
76(L), 76(R), 77(T), 77(R), 78(L), 78(R),
79(L), 79(R), 80, 81(L), 81(CR), 87.
Solo Syndication: p15(B), 38.
South West News: p40/1, 41(TL), 41(TR),
42(T), 42(B), 43, 44(L), 44(R), 45(L), 45(R),
46, 47(L), 47(R).

Every effort has been made to trace the
copyright holders of the photographs in this
book but one or two were unreachable.
We would be grateful if the photographers
concerned would contact us.

Typeset by Capital Setters, London.

Printed in England by Hillingdon Press,
Uxbridge, Middlesex.
This book is dedicated to Daphne,
Mia, Rory-Jamie and Sarah.

contents

THE SUPERSTAR
NEXT DOOR

I think with myself, what I have been able to come up with is being very normal, and everyday people find you easy to relate to and not a threat to them. I do take into account that for a lot of people, pop artists are role models so you have to be careful about what you are doing.

"If I can give my fans enjoyment in some small way, that really makes what I do worthwhile. If I can wave to that group of kids and they go home and talk about it, fantastic, or if I can just sign a measly bit of paper for a kid and he's so stunned he can't talk, that really brings home to me what I am doing it for: because it really makes me feel good."

Life was not always this grand.

Long – well, perhaps not *that* long – ago, in a drowsy Melbourne suburb called Surrey Hills, where Christmas came but once a year and the rest of the time there was the telly, you could say life was dull. Nothing much ever happened in Surrey Hills, and nobody batted an eyelid.

It was not the sort of place you would choose to be born in if you had such a choice, but Kylie Ann Minogue was born there anyway. And the dozy town went about its lethargic business, rarely taking much notice of the oh-so-ordinary little girl in her gingham skirts and plaits. Life, as much as it would in such an uneventful place, carried on regardless.

Then one day, out of the blue there was a miracle – or was it perhaps a fairy tale?

Lady Luck descended on her golden kangaroo, waved her eighteen carat boomerang and whispered the magic words. Little Kylie was whisked out of oblivion and into the far-flung, glittering realm of fame and fortune.

Like Dorothy teetering in her ruby slippers on the brink of the Yellow Brick Road, young Kylie took her first tentative steps towards stardom. Finding her feet, she immersed herself in her role as a Soap Sud with all the ease of a small screen veteran. Still riding the crest of that

"If I can give my fans enjoyment in some small way, that really makes what I do worthwhile."

foaming wave, she took up a microphone one day and sang an old classic, which caught the ear of a sharp record producer who would very soon launch her as a pop star.

At just about the same time, a cigar-gnawing chief executive thousands of miles away was shredding his meticulously planned TV schedules to find a slot for a homely Australian series which was to become one of the all time surprise hits, turning many of its stars into instant celebrities.

One of them more than most.

One minute a mere tomboy Neighbour with a habit of putting a spanner in the works, the next Kylie was an overnight sensation, a pop princess with the Midas touch, so ordinary and yet so electrifying.

And now the gingham frocks and plaits are long forgotten. From her aureole of spun-gold hair to her perfectly lacquered toenails, Kylie is every inch a star. She only has to wear an outfit once for it to become an instant fashion trend. She only has to express a hint of yearning for a food, fad or fantasy for her fans to start racing after them too. What started out as a loyal band of Kylie watchers has now grown into a legion of Wannabes: teenage girls who spend all their waking hours trying to dress, talk and sing like Kylie. They all wannabe like her.

There is no end to the appeal either. Adored by kids, Mums, Dads, Grandmums and Grandads alike, she can do no wrong.

And shrewd businesswoman that she has quickly become, she is milking the phenomenon for all it is worth. For there is, after all, another side of Kylie. On the Grimm, dark side of the fairytale hides an aspect the fawning fans never see. Behind that ordinary, playful tomboy who loves to dress up and paint her face is a tough cookie, with one eye on her bank account.

Everyone admires her for working so hard, for thrashing herself relentlessly to entertain the troops and keep the fans happy. But look closely through those softly parted, glossy lips and you'll notice the perfect teeth set hard and fast in a calculating smile. This is the ruthless side of Kylie, the hard-nosed accountant's daughter who has exploited her popularity to the hilt and capitalised on her success like no other pop star in the past decade. 1990? This is just the beginning.

Madonna has often talked of her Ten Year Plan, a route to megastardom designed to keep her in the manner to which she has quickly become accustomed for years to come too.

But Kylie now eclipses even the Material Girl. Hers is perhaps a 30 year plan, a code that will keep her name in neon until her teenage fans are getting on for grandparenthood and Madonna is another has-been.

It will take more than a streak of dogged determination to see it through. Some say she has learned her lesson well. Others, that she must have been born with it. Who would have thought it possible in a boring little town like Surrey Hills? Down there, of course, Kylie is just the Superstar Next Door.

TO THE LAND
OF OPPORTUNITY

*"One day I'm gonna
be a star."*

For the 13 year old Australian schoolgirl, the trip to London was one of the highlights of her visit to Britain.

For months, back home in Melbourne, she had wondered what The Big City on the other side of the world would look like. Finally, she was here. Along with her mother and British relatives, she took in the sights. Tower Bridge, Buckingham Palace, Trafalgar Square passed by in a whirl of excitement.

But later there was one part of the visit that she was always to remember. A trip to the famous wax works museum Madame Tussaud's. Inside The Hall of Fame she gazed at statues of pop legends like The Beatles, Elton John and her childhood favourites, Abba. She wanted to prod them and gaze into their eyes to check they weren't real. They were superstars every one of them. People queued just to look at their image.

"One day I'm going to be famous, too," she vowed silently. "One day I'm going to be a star."

Eight years later, to be precise, she was greeted by screaming crowds and the flash of a hundred photographers' cameras. She was back at Madame Tussaud's to see her own likeness unveiled in the world's most celebrated Hall of Fame.

At just 21, Kylie Minogue was a star.

Kylie's very first taste of public, or semi public, adoration came on May 28, 1968 in the maternity ward of Melbourne's Bethlehem Hospital. For mum Carol and dad Ron it was their first child and they were absolutely delighted. Kylie Ann Minogue weighed in at just over 6lbs and was immediately established as the darling not only for the Minogues and their friends, but of mum Carol's network of relatives who had emigrated with her from Wales to Australia. As a baby she earned the dubious nickname of anklebiter after trailing around after mum and grabbing at her legs.

Kylie was born into a safe, secure and typical middle class Australian family. But the Kylie story really starts thousands of miles away from Bethlehem Hospital, way down in the Welsh valleys . . .

In 1955, after months of agonizing, Dennis and Millie Jones finally made the momentous decision that they would leave the security of tiny Maesteg in Mid Glamorgan and head for a new life on the other side of the world. Millie's brother, Dennis Riddiford and his wife Joan, also decided to emigrate. Australia may as well have been on another planet to post war Britain. And for thousands it represented a real land of opportunity where the sun shone and the good life was there for the taking. Britain was still recovering from the long hard years of the second World War and the population had long felt the pinch of rationing and having to make do.

But even so, for the Jones and the Riddifords it was a terrible wrench to leave the rest of the close knit Welsh family behind and there were floods of tears when the time came to say goodbye. For young Carol Jones, just eleven years old, it was a terrifying and wonderful time.

The Jones family set sail for a new life. Kylie's mum Carol with short blonde hair is front left

A whole new life was about to begin.

That new life had barely begun however when the family's Australian adventure was hit by heartbreak.

While Dennis and Millie and the first four of their children, Jean, Carol, Suzette and Noel, had headed for the prosperous southern city of Melbourne, Dennis and Joan Riddiford decided to try their luck in the tougher climate of Cairns, in northern Queensland. Through hard work and sheer determination, Dennis carved out a career in the building industry. He was eventually rewarded with work on a prestigious construction project in New Guinea. He was sent to the remote town of Weewak – scene of one of the Japanese forces' final stands in World War II – where a new European Hospital was being built to help the impoverished natives.

But the Riddifords good fortune ran out when, soon after work began, Dennis was taken ill. At first doctors believed he was suffering from little more than sunstroke. The humid heat of the New Guinea forest had probably proven too much for someone used to the dank climate of south Wales, they reassured Joan.

But despite flying Dennis back to the more forgiving climate of Cairns, his fever showed no signs of leaving him. "Eventually the doctors told us that he had black water fever or malaria," remembered Joan.

The medical experts advice was that the searing Australian heat would simply be too much for Dennis. He would have to return to a cooler part of the world.

So it was that just seven years after leaving Wales full of dreams of a lucrative new life, Dennis and Joan were forced to fly back to Glamorgan. The family's gamble in moving to a new world had been tragically soured. The break up opened a wound that would take years to heal. But if anything the cloud hanging over them after the Riddifords left made Dennis, Millie and their expanded family – two more sons Michael and Peter were born after their arrival in Melbourne – even more determined to make it. And make it they did, daughter Suzette succeeding as an actress and eldest son Noel carving out a career as a top TV cameraman.

For Carol Australia proved to be the wonderful country of her dreams. As a teenager Carol looked strikingly like Kylie does now. They have the same sparkling eyes and the same fresh beautiful, face.

Back home in Wales Carol had taken dancing lessons and attended ballet classes. As a teenager, in a little place called Townsville, Carol took the local Theatre Royal by storm. She went on to win a host of medals and trophies. But in her late teens she lost interest. Stardom beyond the like of the Townsville Theatre Royal was not to be.

Carol said: "Basically I was shy. A bit quiet. I never really had the drive or the ambition to go any further. I danced until I was 18 or 19 but then I lost interest.

"I entered a few eisteddfods and competitions and did the exams but that was as far as I went. I think it was a hard life but I loved it while I was doing it."

The premature end to what could have been a professional ballet career meant that Carol at least had more time to devote to the blossoming courtship with a young accountant, Ron Minogue.

At the height of the romance, the pair were inseparable and it was obvious to family and friends that they were heading for the altar. At the wedding a host of best wishes were received from the other side of the world where many relatives called Jones still remembered young Carol who had gone off to Australia as a child and was now all grown up and about to get wed. The marriage was a happy one and when Carol was 24 the couple were blessed with their first child, Kylie Ann.

When Kylie was two, little brother Brendan was born, and a year later Danielle completed the Minogue family.

Growing up in the Melbourne suburbs was, says Kylie, happy, safe and secure. Dad Ron had by now qualified as an accountant and he eventually landed a job with the local council.

Kylie's grandparents Dennis and Millie proudly display their family

In 1973 Kylie was off to the local school, Camberwell primary. There she quickly settled into school life and although she claims to have been "very shy" made lots of friends and impressed the staff with her helpfulness and charm.

"One thing that comes to mind is at kindergarten, though. I remember I had these Smiley boots, which were white vinyl and had Smiley faces on the toes. They were great," remembered Kylie. During those infant years school and home life progressed at an unremarkable pace. The youngster got to watch her favourite shows on television and listen to her favourite groups, like Abba, on the radio.

"I loved *Thunderbirds* – it was just such a weird TV programme – there was nothing else like it. I also loved *The Flintstones*, I wanted to have a car like Fred Flintstone's with my feet poking out of the bottom," said Kylie.

With friends, and sometimes with sister Dannii, Kylie, like millions of youngsters all over the world, acted out her fantasies of pop stardom in front of the bedroom mirror. When asked

Millie with her daughters Carol (left) and Suzette

such a hard life. I wanted them to learn the piano and both did learn. I think the piano is something you have for life. When they started dancing I didn't try and stop them because I had to let them do what they felt was right."

But Carol said she is baffled over how the

Abba: Kylie's childhood heroes

girls came to have such good singing voices. She said: "I can't sing a note. I couldn't even sing in church."

Kylie is very protective of her mother and stresses how close the Minogue family is. One claim guaranteed to draw fire from Kylie is that she missed out on a childhood because of showbiz.

"I don't think so at all. I feel sorry for kids that are in showbusiness from a really young age, people like Shirley Temple. But no, I went through school really normally. So no, I don't think I missed out on anything, I like to think that I gained."

In fact, normal is the best word to describe her childhood. Whenever she speaks of those days, it is with fondness and a smile. Her interests were the same as most young girls the world over – pop music, boys and clothes, not necessarily in that order. At school she was liked

what she wanted to be when she was a child, she admits: "Probably famous, like every other kid. I used to pretend Abba concerts in my bedroom with my friends. We'd put on dresses and dance to Abba records and pretend to be Abba and we would prance about the bedroom or lounge singing into hairbrushes. I wanted to be Agnetha, the blonde one, when I grew up."

Mum Carol encouraged all of her children to express themselves but was never the "pushy showbiz mum". Carol said: "I was never very keen on them taking up dancing because it is

but not considered a leading academic talent.

Said Kylie: "I wasn't really clever but I wasn't stupid. And I was reasonably well behaved. My best friend was a bit of a rascal but I was usually too scared to do anything naughty."

The only hint of rebellion seems to have been sparked by her first crush on a classmate known only by the name Grant. Cheating in a spelling test and playing kiss chase in the playground – it was all down to Grant.

Kylie remembered: "I hope I am better at spelling now than I was then. I remembered the day because I had this huge crush on the boy sitting next to me. When I found out that we had been placed next to each other in class with all my friends around I went, 'Oh no, I'm sitting next to Grant'. But actually I was terribly excited. I was a bit confused about spelling bicycle, about where the 'i' and the 'y' went. So yes, we cheated together. The start of a blossoming romance!"

Sports were not top of the list. Crafts and Arts subjects were Kylie's favourite, especially later at Camberwell High School. "Even back at primary school I was more of a homey, crafty person. I'd rather sit and do something like sewing even if it might be monotonous to someone else. I liked reading rather than, say, going out and playing netball."

In fact, the young Kylie Minogue was just like everybody's favourite girl next door. The kind of girl that even if you didn't know well you always said "hello" to and got a cheery wave and a smile back.

Little did they guess that in a few years' time they would be telling their friends and relatives about the superstar who used to live next door in the suburbs.

chapter two

A CHILD STAR
IS BORN

**Mum Carol during her ballet dancing
days**

For the happy-go-lucky youngster from Surrey Hills, life quite literally took a dramatic turn when she was just 11 years old. Kylie may persist in claiming a numbingly normal childhood, but how many kids of that age get a chance to star on national television?

Up until then Kylie's biggest audience had been an adoring family and friends who watched as she pranced around the lounge impersonating her favourite pop stars. Carol's dancing and her sister Suzette's acting provided the inspiration for the Minogue sisters – Danielle or Dannii as she was known in the clan was also showing signs of talent – and the pair loved nothing better than play acting at home.

But in 1980 the play acting suddenly became real. Kylie had just finished primary school and along with Dannii, got the chance to audition for a part in *The Sullivans*, a long-running soap set in World War II. The big break came via a relative who worked for Crawford Productions, then Australia's biggest producer of television drama.

Carol took her daughters along to the audition expecting Dannii to have the best chance of landing the part of Carla, a young Dutch girl. The outline of the character seemed

right for her youngest daughter but when producer Alan Hardy saw Kylie, it was she he chose.

Kylie remembered: "I had to speak in a Dutch accent which I wasn't very good at." It was good enough however to set her on the way to winning vital experience – and other roles soon followed.

"At the time I also appeared in an episode of the *Skyways* series which didn't last too long because it was pretty dreadful," remembered Kylie. *Skyways*, set in and around an international airport, may well have been "pretty dreadful" but it did bring Kylie into contact with a promising young actor who years later was to take centre stage in her life.

He was Jason Donovan, the son of actor Terence Donovan and actress Sue McIntosh, and in *Skyways* he played Kylie's brother.

After this brief affair with TV, Kylie returned to the classroom where she knuckled down to the job of passing her exams. There was, however, still time for the occasional screen appearance and as she headed towards graduation from High School Kylie popped up in a mini-series, *Fame And Misfortune*, and another show *The Zoo Family*.

It was in 1984, when Kylie was still only 16, that her next big break came and it was again Alan Hardy, the man who had cast her in *The Sullivans* three years before, who was involved. The show was *The Henderson Kids* and Kylie auditioned for the part of Charlotte Kernow – known as Char – in a tomboy role that was to prove remarkably similar to the character that would one day transform her into a superstar.

Alan Hardy said later: "I remember she came in costume for her audition looking a little on the tarty side. She had this wonderful natural and infectious charm. She was clearly number one for Char. When we started filming she was very

shy but she got better as she went along and she picked up confidence. She was very lively with a spark of her own. She is very photogenic but fortunately she knows that being photogenic is not enough in this business."

Her unusually youthful looks meant Kylie could play a girl four years her junior and her portrayal of the spirited 12-year-old Charlene helped make *The Henderson Kids* a hit in Australia. Success was not going to turn her head yet however and Kylie made sure her school work didn't suffer. By the end of 1985 she had passed the Higher School Certificate and was ready to leave Camberwell High.

Despite the impression she had made on television, Kylie was not certain she wanted to stay in acting when she left. She considered taking a "normal" job, perhaps making use of her practical skills. "I would have made a great secretary, I love organising things. I always assumed I'd leave school and get a "proper" job, then get married, have kids and look after my family in a modest little house. And if you had asked my mum and dad whether I had it in me to be an actress or singer they would have laughed you out of town," said Kylie.

"Not that they ever had any great big designs on my future. I don't think they had any real ambitious expectations for any of us as long as we were happy. They never really boasted to their friends like other people's parents sometimes did. You know the stuff . . . 'Oh, when our daughter grows up, she's going to be a barrister'," she added.

"They never made me go to auditions – it was just something that came up. My auntie, my mum's sister Suzette, was an actress."

The adventurous side of Kylie's spirit eventually triumphed though and just a few months after her exams another audition was being set up. Kylie was to audition for the role of a tomboy mechanic called Charlene Mitchell, in a new soap called *Neighbours*. It was a part very close to Char from *The Henderson Kids*. "She was ideal for both. Don't tell me that Charlene in *Neighbours* was very different from *The Hendersons'* Char," said Alan Hardy. Sadly for Kylie though, whether or not she got the most important role she had yet auditioned for did not depend on a man already convinced of her potential.

This time she would have to get past one of Australia's toughest talent spotters, a woman with a reputation for making or breaking young stars. Her name was Jan Russ.

THE STARMAKER

Herself a former actress, Jan Russ played a crucial real life role in shaping Kylie for stardom.

Jan, a divorced mother of a 12 year old son, is regarded as one of the best showbiz talent spotters in Australia.

It was six years ago she was approached and offered a job as casting director for a planned new soap opera . . . *Neighbours.*

She remembers all the Ramsay Street actors and actresses with fondness – Jan also discovered Jason Donovan, who arrived for an audition in his school uniform, and a host of others. But in particular she recalls the time she first saw Kylie.

Jan, who starred as an actress in theatre and musical comedy before taking her first casting job with *Prisoner: C Block H,* smiles when asked how she approaches star spotting.

"Initially it's their looks, their talent, their presence, their own personality, you know like body language, sexuality if you like. I mean talent has obviously got to head the list. They have got to have some natural talent to home in on them, at first.

"Also, that image, I guess with Kylie and Jason particularly they are the type of people that

everybody would like as their daughter or son or granddaughter or niece or nephew. You know they are typical boy and girl next door, I think that has helped their success."

But what Jan was also looking for was someone who could spark off the right romantic chemistry with Jason Donovan. Her instincts told her Kylie was perfect.

"She was right," Jason says now. "There was instantly that feeling between us that probably happens once in a million. You can't make chemistry happen, you can't say: 'You and you are going to be so and so.' You can't manufacture it. There was just this great feeling there."

Though Jan was not initially aware of it, this was not the first time they'd been cast together. Six years earlier they'd played brother and sister in another soap opera, *Skyways.* Kylie recalls that at the time, "Jason was really chubby with a bowl haircut and I was really small with straight blonde hair."

It was the friendship that developed in those early days which added to the success of Jan's casting. "I think the feeling between us had a lot to do with *Skyways* and the contact we had early

on," says Jason.

Physically both had changed – so much so that Jason didn't recognise Kylie at first. "She came into the van and said she was the new person on the block or whatever – and bang – there she was," Jason recalls.

"She said: 'You remember don't you?' and I said 'Yeah'. But I wasn't too sure. Then I remembered her face. It was pretty weird."

It was not *Skyways,* though, that Jan remembered Kylie from. In between Kylie had enjoyed success in a few other minor television roles. In particular Jan had been impressed with Kylie after seeing her on *The Zoo Family.*

"She was playing a bit of a commonish type girl, with really short mini skirts and all this. When the role of Charlene came up, I remembered her and called her in with some others. Annie Jones, who plays Jane, was also in the running. But Kylie had just the right look and style and character. Just as I imagined it."

When Jan first saw the fresh faced youngster – by now 18 years old – there was never any doubt that she was the actress for the role of Charlene.

"I just knew she was right for the role. It's strange you have an image in your mind of the particular person you want for the particular role. Somehow when that person comes on the screen you know immediately, that's right, that's the one, they really make the character come to life.

"But at the time I don't think Kylie or anybody else had any idea of the phenomenal success she would have. None of us expected it to go to the proportions it has gone to. Other Australian shows have played in England but they haven't achieved the success this one has."

Jan, in common with others who have

worked with Kylie, is quick to praise her professionalism and common sense, and she also tries to put her finger on that little something which makes a real star.

"In Kylie's case, she had a certain spark, that something extra. Also she photographed beautifully. The camera adores her and she has this wonderful presence that comes through the camera lens. She has an extra charisma, or whatever you like to call it. It just comes through. You just see her on camera and she has this wonderful something."

For all that Jan remembers the off screen Kylie as vulnerable and not in the least spoiled by her success. "In real life she's a shy little thing. She's a young girl who really has her feet planted on the ground and I don't believe she has let herself be carried away by her success. And more than this she's sensible enough to know that her success may not last forever.

"She's a lovely kid and I think she's handled herself extremely well for someone of her age. She's only 21 and she's crammed a lot into a very short space of time."

Jan smiles at the memory of Kylie. Wandering around the cavernous warehouse that contains the *Neighbours* sets in Nunawading, Melbourne, she fondly points out various props which have all played a part in shaping the history of Ramsay Street.

"This," said Jan taking a seat on top of a rolled up patterned carpet, "was Kylie Minogue's bedroom carpet – or Charlene's, I should say."

She is fiercely proud of the achievements of the cast and obviously misses the ones that have left – particularly Kylie and Jason. She remembers both of them with fondness and pride.

"I remember when Jason first came and auditioned for me one day after school in his school uniform, very hot and perspiring, and a typical teenage schoolboy who had just run to the audition.

"He turned down the part I offered him then – which was the best thing he ever did. Two years later after he'd finished his studies he came back and claimed the part of Scott.

"Boy, oh boy," Jan jokes, "Kylie and Jason – those two were really something, weren't they?

"If I'd had any sense at all I would have signed them up for ten years or fifteen per cent . . . !"

BOYFRIENDS AND BEST FRIENDS

Boyfriends, for a young and pretty girl like Kylie, were never a problem. She is the first to admit that she was bitten by the Puppy Love bug from quite an early age – which stood her in good stead when it came to dealing with the opposite sex in later years.

"I fell in love for the first time while I was still at school," she has revealed. "When I was in grade three I had a crush on this really big guy. I can't think of his name now, but it was great because there was this really tough girl who wanted to hang around with me because this guy fancied me. This was one way of getting girlfriends! But you know what? I wouldn't know him if I tripped over him now."

He would hardly be likely to say the same thing about Kylie. In fact he probably stands a round of beers with his mates every now and then on the strength of his unrequited schoolboy romance with a fluffy little classmate who grew up into a sexy, albeit pintsized superstar.

Kylie never tires of telling interviewers that life at home at Camberwell High School was just as normal as it could possibly be. And that included a few classroom crushes. Another early romance, which Kylie has often spoken

Friendly fun? Kylie and Jason have been inseparable since their teens

about, was with the infamous Grant. His last name may not be known, but there is a place in Kylie history for the ten year old who managed to sweep her off her feet.

They cheated in a spelling test together and they played kiss chase in the playground. And as Kylie admits: "I had a huge crush on Grant. I used to slow down when we played kiss chase so Grant could catch me!"

Like most romances involving ten year olds, it was destined not to last the fifth grade. Kylie progressed from Camberwell's infant section into the senior school and, at least romantically, left Grant behind.

At home the young Kylie, with kid sister

Danielle and brother Brendan, would go on family outings, often to the movies. These were family treats particularly enjoyed by the starstruck sisters who would sit silently for hours lost in the fantasy of the silver screen.

After a visit to see *Grease*, the girls were particularly impressed with stars John Travolta and Australian-born Olivia Newton-John. And Kylie confessed later that she liked nothing better than to "pretend" she was in a pop group like Abba, prancing around her bedroom holding a hairbrush as a microphone.

Kylie laughs when she recalls herself dancing around the Minogue living room singing 'Greased Lightning' for family and friends. Sister Dannii would often join in and little could parents Carol and Ron have realised just where this extrovert show of singing and dancing would lead to.

Kylie would spend hours listening to the radio, singing or humming along the latest hits. Often she would also spend hours designing and making new clothes for herself and sometimes for Dannii and friends.

By the time she was in senior school her love of fashion was firmly established. Friends at Camberwell were often impressed by Kylie's wardrobe and a few realised her secret – she had made most of the outfits herself.

One former boyfriend recalled that Kylie could "run up an outfit in two hours". But in a television interview at the end of 1989 Kylie confessed that the pressures of international stardom meant that now she has precious little time to spare for making her own clothes.

Kylie said: "I used to design all my own clothes when I was younger, when I was 15, 16. Now I like wearing Australian clothes – I say that not wearing anything Australian at this particular moment – but there are lots of really good young Australian designers."

The fashionably turned out Kylie caught the eye of many boys at Camberwell. And handsome David Wood, who now runs his own hairdressing salon in Melbourne, was lucky enough to date her.

David and his pals spent long summer days at the local swimming pool and they were out to impress the girls. Kylie and her best friend Georgina Adamson also visited the pool. According to David, the couple were soon courting.

In an interview he recalled that Kylie was great fun to be with but she was not keen on spending too much time at parties or discos.

Like any other young couple they teamed up for outings to the beach, for barbecues with friends, or visits to the cinema. They would sit and talk for hours about what they would do when they left school.

At times Kylie, who had already appeared on television by then, would talk of her hopes for fame. And others would speak of an "ordinary" job like a secretary.

David said in an interview: "She always wanted to be famous, always saying 'I want to be a star'. Not in acting . . . in pop. Or else with her own line in fashion clothes. She was always ace on a sewing machine. She could knock up an outfit in two hours."

The couple met when David was 14 and Kylie a year younger. The romance finally ended when Kylie won her biggest break, the role of Charlene in *Neighbours*. Whispers of a blossoming romance with her handsome co-star, Jason Donovan, had already surfaced. But it was the gruelling work schedule Kylie was now working which placed the greatest strain according to friends.

David said: "Kylie told me she wanted our romance to end because she had a lot of pressure from work – she was always very busy."

The demanding schedule of a soap meant that Kylie was often working 12 hours a day and spending what little time she had left in the evening reading her script.

But they remain firm friends, and David has nothing but praise for the way his former girlfriend has handled stardom. "She is not big headed at all," he says. "She talks more about the stars she has met than what she has done."

"She wasn't really much of a party goer, she hated nightclubs and she frowned on drinking and smoking."

Sister Dannii, best friend to young Kylie

chapter five

I SHOULD BE SO LUCKY

It was in the summer of 1987 that Kylie's pop career was launched. And luck, a commodity the spirited teenager had never been short of, played a crucial part in the events that were to set her on the path to millions.

Music had always played an important part in the lives of the Minogue family. With mum Carol's heritage it could never have been any other way – her roots, after all, lay thousands of miles away in Wales, the Land of Song. As children Kylie and sister Dannii spent many lost hours singing into their bedroom mirrors. If – hairbrush microphones in hand – they were not pretending to be Abba, it was Welsh star Bonnie Tyler who was the inspiration for their unenthusiastic warblings. Carol and Ron encouraged the duo – even if they were baffled as to where their talent had come from.

"I can't sing a note. I couldn't even sing in church. But my father's cousin was head of the conservatorium in Wales, so I suppose it is somewhere in the family blood," confessed Carol. To Kylie and Dannii, their music was simply fun. Innocent, harmless enjoyment.

"Whenever I used to feel on top of the world, I would just open my mouth and sing,

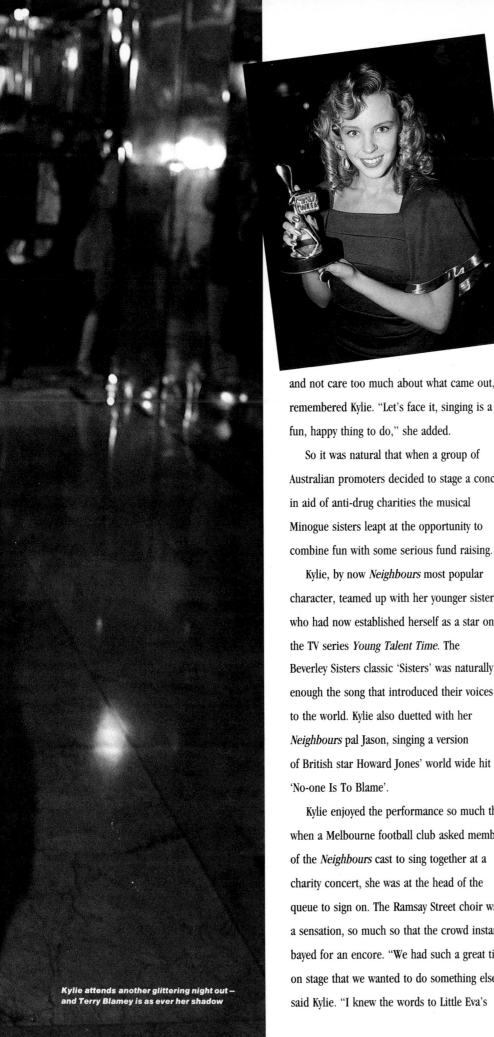

and not care too much about what came out,"
remembered Kylie. "Let's face it, singing is a
fun, happy thing to do," she added.

So it was natural that when a group of
Australian promoters decided to stage a concert
in aid of anti-drug charities the musical
Minogue sisters leapt at the opportunity to
combine fun with some serious fund raising.

Kylie, by now *Neighbours* most popular
character, teamed up with her younger sister
who had now established herself as a star on
the TV series *Young Talent Time*. The
Beverley Sisters classic 'Sisters' was naturally
enough the song that introduced their voices
to the world. Kylie also duetted with her
Neighbours pal Jason, singing a version
of British star Howard Jones' world wide hit
'No-one Is To Blame'.

Kylie enjoyed the performance so much that
when a Melbourne football club asked members
of the *Neighbours* cast to sing together at a
charity concert, she was at the head of the
queue to sign on. The Ramsay Street choir was
a sensation, so much so that the crowd instantly
bayed for an encore. "We had such a great time
on stage that we wanted to do something else,"
said Kylie. "I knew the words to Little Eva's

'The Locomotion', the backing was simple and
the band knew the song, so we raced out and
did an impromptu performance," she added.

It was then that Lady
Luck once more shone on Kylie. One of
Australia's sharpest young record bosses, Gary
Ashley, of Mushroom Records saw Kylie's
performance. He persuaded her to record a
version of the song – and the rest became
Australian recording history.

Mike Duffy, a sound engineer with Britain's
most successful production team of Stock,
Aitken and Waterman, heard Kylie's rendition
of the song and re-recorded it for Mushroom.
Kylie's disco version of 'The Locomotion' was
released in July 1987. It went on to top the
charts for eight incredible weeks. And it became
the best selling single of not only the year but of
the decade in Australia.

"This is fantastic. I have to keep pinching
myself to believe it's happening," said an
incredulous Kylie as her singing career dawned.
What was to follow would leave the world
pinching itself. The success of 'The Locomotion'
confirmed what Gary Ashley's instincts had
already told him. But to consolidate Kylie's
breakthrough he knew there was only one place
to take her – to London and Stock, Aitken and
Waterman's already legendary hit factory. So it
was that during a week long break from filming
Neighbours in October 1987 Kylie boarded an
airliner and left the sweltering sunshine of
Melbourne for the cold and rain of an English
autumn. At Kylie's side for that crucial trip was
the man that her father Ron had just chosen
to oversee her career. Commerce graduate
Terry Blamey had won himself a reputation
as one of Australia's brightest entertainment

entrepreneurs with his company Pace Entertainment. Kylie's astute accountant father had been particularly impressed by Blamey's management of stars like Mark 'Jacko' Jackson. His instructions to Blamey were to do even better for his eldest daughter.

When he arrived with Kylie in London, however, Blamey could have been forgiven for thinking his relationship with the Minogues was to be a short one. Stock, Aitken and Waterman's achievements in the four years since they had joined forces were – even in an industry known for its hyperbole – sensational. The trio – musicians Mike Stock and Matt Aitken, and talent spotter cum marketing mastermind Pete Waterman – had revolutionised Britain's record industry. Based in a back alley recording studio in an unfashionable part of the city, they had married their talents to perfect a pop formula that was selling millions. Their distinctive, disco orientated sound had been a vehicle for the launch of a series of stars, from Princess and Sinitta to Rick Astley.

The trio – all of whom had at one time endured menial jobs in factories, Stock making gaskets, Aitken fizzy drinks and Waterman manufacturing telephone dials – were now at the helm of the 1980's most phenomenal Hit Factory. "We come in every day and instead of gaskets or lemonade, we are turning out hits. As far as we are concerned it is exactly the same thing," said Mike Stock. "We are no different from people like Mozart and Shakespeare. Mozart wrote music so he could buy himself velvet trousers and Shakespeare got up to write a play every day because he needed to live like the rest of us," he added with the disarming arrogance that had established him as one-third of pop's most hated team.

Kylie and her new Svengali Blamey got an instant glimpse of that arrogance when they turned up on the doorstep of the Hit Factory. To Stock, Aitken and Waterman she was an unknown Australian singer from a then unknown Australian soap opera. Despite Mike Duffey's testimonial and the success of 'The Locomotion' in Australia she hadn't yet earned the right to be taken too seriously.

Kylie and Blamey were forced to wait agonising days before the trio agreed to sit down and talk about writing a song. And it was only on the final day of their trip to London that the Hit Men took the tiny teenager into the recording studio. But if Kylie and Blamey had started to harbour doubts over the wisdom of their journey, they were instantly dispelled when the men with the Midas touch began work.

Matt Aitken walked into the studio armed with just an idea. "She's come to make a hit, she should be so lucky," the trio had joked as a nervous Kylie had sat patiently waiting to see them. Aitken began mapping out the song that was to be one of the biggest hits of the 1980s. Handing Kylie lyrics line by line, 'I Should Be So Lucky' began to form. And Kylie, singing like she had never before, grasped the moment.

"We were rather brusque and offhand with her when she came in that first time," Waterman remembered. "If she didn't learn a lesson, we certainly did," he added.

Masters of their art, Stock, Aitken and Waterman realised that day they had unearthed a talent that could outshine anything, even in their empire. But they had to wait for a host of their rivals to commit pop suicide before they could begin the job of moulding this new discovery.

Ashley and Mushroom Records wanted Kylie's new song released under licence to a major British record company. But amazingly every company approached rejected Kylie. No-one in Britain knew yet how *Neighbours* was about to take hold of the nation, but many also turned down Kylie, telling her management . . . "Sorry but she can't sing."

Musical history will remember those rejections, ranking them with the men from Decca Records who early in the 1960s said 'No' to Brian Epstein and his promising newcomers The Beatles.

Pete Waterman, however, was prepared to gamble. His unerring instinct told him his company had stumbled across something special and he released 'I Should Be So Lucky' on his own PWL label. He astutely formed a joint venture with Mushroom Records too. PAL Productions would handle Kylie's recording rights around the rest of the world.

"I'm going to make you the new Madonna," Waterman promised his new prodigy, but even today he shakes his head disbelievingly at the opportunity others missed. "I couldn't believe it. No-one would entertain her," said Waterman, remembering the snubs Kylie received. Waterman's judgement proved – once again – perfect when the single was released. 'I Should Be So Lucky' shot to number one, not just in Britain and Australia but in 16 other countries besides.

From Finland to Hong Kong – where also no-one had even heard of Charlene Mitchell – Kylie became a sensation. As her record sold in millions and she began to entertain ideas of being a full time pop star for the first time, Kylie knew who she had to thank. "It's all down to Stock, Aitken and Waterman," she said. "I'm just a beginner, they are the guys with all the experience. I'm not even sure what my musical style is. I love the songs they write for me and I try to make it look that way in the style in which I deliver it," she added modestly. "Now as I progress I hope to develop musically. I don't know what my future style will be but the one thing I do know is that it will keep on changing."

Kylie quickly followed up the success of 'I Should Be So Lucky' with another single, 'Got To Be Certain'. It proved a certain hit and shot to number two in the UK before topping the charts in Belgium, Australia, Hong Kong and Finland, and storming top tens all across Europe.

Criticism, though, was bound to raise its ugly head, and so it did. And it was her fellow Australians who plunged in the knives with most relish. Several top Australian radio stations refused to play 'I Should Be So Lucky', claiming it had a "high irritant factor". Some declared Minogue-free zones and preferred to play a spoof record instead, 'I Should Be So Yucky'. The Australian press dubbed her the 'Singing Budgie' and 'I hate Kylie' T-shirts appeared on the streets in their hundreds.

For Kylie, however, there was no looking back, and the future for now meant more work with SAW in London where she was to record an album as soon as her *Neighbours* commitments allowed. Mike Stock, the most cerebral of the hit making trio, was already convinced Kylie was a unique talent. He couldn't wait for her return to the Hit Factory. "She's not the sort of girl who wants to make political statements with her music. She doesn't want to

The Hitmen. Matt Aitken, Pete Waterman, and Mike Stock

"I'm going to make you the next Madonna."

wear black," he said.

"She wants to pass on the message that the world is still a great place despite everything. It's not just hype, but she is a joy to work with too. Unlike some singers, she has an inbuilt discipline. She will listen and learn very quickly. You hear of actresses being temperamental – this girl isn't. She is a realist through and through. She's self-assured and she knows where she is going in life," he added.

As the trio began mapping out the songs that would fill Kylie's first album, Stock was among the first to make what was to become a familiar prediction. "She is no short term flash in the pan. We hope we are still working with her when she is thirty – if she still wants us then. In the meantime, we have been very lucky to have her . . . "

JUST ANOTHER BIMBETTE?

he backstreet warehouse, buried in the faceless sprawl of south London, was far enough removed from the searing, eighty degree heat of Kylie's favourite Port Philip Bay beach. But on a rainy March afternoon in 1988 it must have seemed a million miles from home.

Quick-on-the-uptake pro that she was fast becoming though, Kylie put a brave face on it as she began the slow – and often painful – process of consolidating her success. "Refreshing," she euphemistically called the British climate she was about to face for the first time as a "star".

"And it's great to be here working with Stock, Aitken and Waterman. It's a dream for me to be here making an album with them," she added as she arrived in the UK five months after her visit to record 'I Should Be So Lucky'. Her words belied the apprehension she undoubtedly harboured over facing her biggest test yet.

Kylie had returned to PWL's Hit Factory behind Borough tube station on the south side of the Thames two miles from the City of London, to record her début album. 'I Should Be So Lucky' had topped the UK charts for a

(Left): Kylie outside the Hit Factory during recording of her début album

"We were genuinely worried we were going to get 200,000 kids outside the front door, she's becoming so popular."

Family girl. Mum Carol, Kylie's "stabilising influence" is an almost constant companion

remarkable five weeks, selling 698,000 copies. The breakthrough had been made but now was the time to confirm her arrival as a major talent.

When she last flew into London no one would have noticed the elfin-formed teenager drift through customs. This time however, PR machine wheels oiled in advance, fully-briefed paparazzi lay in wait at Heathrow, and from then on menacing minders followed Kylie's every delicate footstep.

As they began work on the new songs Mike Stock had mapped out for their latest discovery, the world's most successful record producing trio explained they now realised what they had on their hands. "We are genuinely worried that we are going to get 200,000 kids outside our front door, she's becoming so popular," said Waterman dressed as ever in sharp shirt, and jeans. Pointing at the three musclemen positioned outside his HQ's entrance, he added: "We'd be stupid not to have these guys around at the moment."

Cocooned inside fortress PWL, Kylie chose her first interviews in Britain to explain the homespun philosophy that was to keep body and soul together during this trying two months

in Britain.

Dressed casually in button-down-collared shirt, faded denims and suede cowboy boots, she sat behind the mixing console of one of PWL's studios and said: "My parents are fantastic, they are the stabilising influence in my life.

"It is very hard for me to comprehend what is happening to me at home in Australia let alone here in Britain and around the world. But I know they are there, along with my sister Danielle and brother Brendan, and it is a great source of strength for me.

"I think success is all about positive vibes – and they are all a very positive influence on me, while at the same time never being pushy.

"I know what I am getting into. I believe in the tall poppy syndrome that if you grow up too tall there will always be people ready to cut you down to size. I think that is a stupid thing to do, but it is a fact that it happens.

"I want to grow and develop as a person in areas that I have not explored yet. I know that I could suffer in that way but I hope I will be able to cope," she added.

Her instant success as a recording artist had, however, crystallised one thought in Kylie's head. *Neighbours*, the show that was her launch pad, might have to be jettisoned. She was given extended leave from the show by bosses at Grundy, who were already losing the battle to persuade her to stay on as Charlene. But with the album scheduled for a summer launch, Kylie signalled that she was already preparing to leave.

"I got the role in *Neighbours* soon after I finished High School. I was originally going to do between one and 12 weeks on it, but now I've been there two and half years," she said.

"My singing career sort of got off the ground through the show too because it was when a few of us from the show got together to sing at a benefit concert for a football club in Australia that I first publicly sang 'The Locomotion.'

"It was just about the only song I knew the words to and was an impromptu thing, but it got things started. "I owe the show a lot obviously, but my contract is up for renewal in June this year and I will have to think about it seriously then. It could be time to leave, but we shall see," she confided.

"All I can say though is that whatever happens it will be my decision," she said, revealing the determination and single-mindedness that was later to be turned against her.

Kylie used that first trip to Britain to indulge, with mother Carol, her passion for shopping. "I've already taken her to Harrods. I have a real weakness for clothes and I like my mum to help me choose them," she said.

Kylie the quasi-intellectual also made an appearance. While thousands of miles away her countrymen were revelling in the celebrations for Australia's 200th anniversary, she enjoyed the historic sights of a country with a slightly richer heritage.

"I have always been interested in art and history since High School. I did art right up until the end of school and have always had an interest in architecture. I want to see as much of London and the rest of Britain as I can while I am here. Back home they are celebrating 200 years but that seems nothing compared to here.

"Your architecture reflects the history too, you have things like Roman walls and roads, we have nothing like that," she added.

As the relentless publicity machinery of pop set about building Kylie into the perfectly-packaged star, however, the cerebral was taking a back seat to the sensational.

Like every creation of the music business, Kylie relied on hype and headlines to stoke up interest in her and her music. And by the spring of 1988, the column inches devoted to her in Britain's tabloids were adding up to miles.

First there were the stories that Kylie was in fact a complete fabrication. 'I Should Be So Lucky' had in reality been sung by Stock, Aitken and Waterman's then golden boy Rick Astley. All the master puppeteers of pop had done was speed up the sophisticated, satin-smooth voice of the boy from Newton-le-Willows in Lancashire to end up with the higher-pitched, female version – Kylie.

Then there were the stories of her rows with jealous younger sister Dannii, and her painful ordeal suffering from the slimmers' disease anorexia nervosa. There was also the story, this time true, that she had splashed out $250,000 on a luxury home in the suburbs of her native Melbourne, only to rent it out while she stayed at home with her beloved parents.

"I chose it myself, but I can't bring myself to live there just yet," she explained when asked about the four bedroomed apartment. "For now it is a good investment," she added shrewdly.

Already though, by far the most persistent story centred on her relationship with her *Neighbours* co-star and long-time 'best friend' Jason Donovan.

During her first public visit to Britain, Kylie set the tone for two years of teasing and tantalising. "Yes we are friends, we have known each other since we were both 12 years old and we do spend lots of time together," she said.

"But there is no truth in these stories that we are romantically linked. At the moment I am just too busy for boyfriends. I am only 19 and there are lots of years ahead of me. For now I want to devote my all to what I am doing now. I

"There's nothing wrong with pop stars coming from all over the world is there?"

would like to have a family one day but I cannot think about next week, let alone something as important as that," she added with already familiar coyness.

Kylie's emergence as a pop star coincided with the arrival of a handful of other girls at the upper end of the charts. Like her they were teenagers, like her they had enjoyed a smash hit first single, like her they happened to have come from somewhere other than Britain. But comparisons with France's Vanessa Paradis who had a hit with 'Joe Le Taxi', Tiffany from America who topped the charts with 'I Think We're Alone Now' and New Yorker Debbie Gibson who broke through with her single 'Shake Your Love', were greeted with scorn by their Antipodean rival.

And suggestions that she was part of a virginal vanguard of "bimbettes" – too young and unsullied to be fully-fledged bimbos – brought the first flashes of what was to become a formidable temper.

"There's nothing wrong with pop stars coming from all over the world is there? And in the past pop has been dominated by groups and men singers," protested Kylie.

"And as for the idea that I am being some how manipulated all I can say is that I don't know about the other girls but I have been in a similar industry – television, for the last couple of years and now I know how it works.

"There are people out there who want to use you and then just throw you away when they have finished with you. I don't intend that to happen to me.

"I intend to stay in control – and I will make my own decisions all the way."

Those words proved to be much more than plain fighting talk.

G'BYE RAMSAY STREET

(Right): The Ramsay Street
Clan. The Neighbours
cast Kylie missed so much

The end of phase one of Kylie Minogue's unstoppable rise to world fame came on a sunny afternoon in June 1988. It was then, with typical "so what" understatement on screen, tomboyish, trouble-making Charlene left *Neighbours*, the show that has made Kylie a part of everyday mythology in both hemispheres.

Charlene's last appearance came in episode 777 of the saga of the warring tribes of Ramsay Street, when she left to set up home in Brisbane with her young husband Scott, played by Jason Donovan. The script was left open by straw-clutching executives at Grundy TV who were still clinging vainly to the hope that their biggest audience puller might one day return.

For Kylie, however, there was to be no looking back. Within a month of filming the episode she flew back to London – heart of her new global empire – where she planned record and film work designed to guarantee that soon she would never need to work in Ramsay Street – or anywhere else for that matter – again.

"I certainly don't degrade *Neighbours* and I know that I owe Charlene everything. Without her I wouldn't be here," she admitted at the time. "But now I want to improve my acting by tackling more demanding roles. I want to go forward," she said.

The confidence of those words confirmed that in two and a half years *Neighbours* – the show which baffled the critics as its banality won millions of fans around the world – had transformed the shy, diffident Kylie into an unashamedly ambitious young woman.

The turning point came when, thousands of miles away from the series' Melbourne home, the then controller of the BBC's main channel ripped up his schedules in a bid to beat plunging ratings. The flamboyant, cigar smoking Michael Grade bowed to postbag pressure from teenage TV watchers who were demanding that the "Down Under Soap" recently introduced to the UK should be switched from its mid-morning slot to the early evening schedule.

Grade decided that the complaints from parents and teachers that kids were arriving late in class because of the series – not to mention that nagging suspicion that placing *Neighbours* on before the evening's news bulletin could be a ratings coup – should be ignored no longer. His move, in January 1988, turned out to be one of the scheduling masterstrokes of the '80s, and within months the soap's ratings had soared towards the 20 million mark and the top of the TV charts.

Critics, educationalists and sociologists tried in vain to explain the appeal of a show in which the birth of a puppy would rate as the event of the week. But while the experts complained about the way 'soft soap' was sterilising British brains, only to then argue that on the other hand *Neighbours* was "allowing more public expressions of family emotions", Kylie was taking full advantage of the situation.

*"I owe Charlene everything.
Without her I wouldn't
be here."*

Kylie with screen mum Ann Charleston

Stock, Aitken and Waterman had taken her under their protective wing and such master opportunists didn't need any convincing that the success of the soap could be translated into success in the record business. Together with Kylie's talent and ambition, the situation offered a recipe for riches beyond even their wildest dreams.

Kylie's departure was an emotional affair for almost everyone at Grundy, the modest television company that never really grasped *Neighbours* worldwide success. Grundy rescued it for the Channel 10 network after it had proved a massive flop on rival Channel 7.

"We all remember it well. It was episode number 777. When filming was over there was a little party, a few speeches and a lot of tears. It was very moving for all of us," remembered Grundy's publicist Kerrie Theobald.

Kylie shed as many tears as anyone, she recalled. "Grundy picked up the series after Channel 7 dropped it in 1985. We went on the air in October 1986 and Kylie joined the cast about four months into the series. She did five episodes a week for the first two years but then began to ease up after her record career began to take off. In many ways Kylie grew up with us on *Neighbours* so everyone understood what it meant when she left. We were always a very close bunch of people," she said.

Two of the leading members of the cast confirmed that – far from being glad to see the back of Kylie as some reports had suggested – there was sadness over her departure. "The thing is that most of us were good friends, many of us still are. I've been thirty years in the business and this is the one place I have been where there are no petty jealousies or anything like that. We always try to help each other,"

said one of Kylie's closest cast friends, Ian Smith, who plays the bumbling Harold Bishop in the series.

He was backed by the grand dame of the series, Ann Charleston, who plays the matriarchal Madge. "Most of us think a great deal of both Kylie and Jason Donovan. *Neighbours* has been a springboard for a lot of careers, especially kids like them," she said.

Kylie herself remembers the day she filmed her 542nd episode of *Neighbours* as being one of the worst of her otherwise happy life. "I thought I was going to bawl my eyes out and I did," she confessed.

"I know that a lot of people think I am made of steel. But I'm not, I'm only human," she added.

At the root of the mixture of emotions that Kylie felt that day was the very real fear that despite the fame and fabulous wealth that might lie ahead of her, her future might not allow her to ever again be part of as precious and close a group of friends as she was during her *Neighbours* days.

A triumvirate of male stars – Jason, Alan Dale and Ian Smith – were the most supportive friends in her life and the still nervous 20-year-old was scared she might not replace them. Certainly Stock, Aitken and Waterman and the guardian angel figure of manager Terry Blamey were waiting in the wings, but would they understand and care for her in the same way?

"I cried because I knew when I walked out on Ramsay Street, it would be a hundred times more difficult to see my friends," she confessed. And of Jason, Alan and Ian she said; "They were all incredibly supportive to me. They were like boyfriends, brothers, fathers and uncles

Anne Haddy and Alan Dale

Kylie's departure was an emotional affair for almost everyone at Grundy.

rolled into one. I'll never forget them for what they did for me and I'll miss them all terribly," she added.

Positive as ever, however, Kylie did admit to looking forward to one element of her new found freedom. She could finally drop her hated nickname Bruiser!

"I used to be called Shorty all through school because I am so small. But the *Neighbours* crew dubbed me Bruiser after a scene in which I was supposed to hit Jason," she said.

"A stunt co-ordinator showed me how to do a fake punch. But I accidentally hit Jason full on the jaw so hard that I knocked him over. He was very brave about the whole thing, crawling up to his feet and telling me it didn't hurt a bit.

"But months later he confessed that it had hurt like hell," she said.

Within four weeks of filming her final episode and saying goodbye to her friends at Grundy, Kylie was based in London where she was now enjoying the sort of stardom attention reserved for Madonna and Michael Jackson.

Her third single – SAW's version of her old favourite, Little Eva's 'The Loco-Motion', – had soared to the number two slot maintaining her record of getting her releases in the top two. Her management – under the Svengali-like leadership of agent Terry Blamey – capitalised with a succession of public appearances and chat show interviews, including a lavish champagne party to launch her first LP, called simply 'Kylie'.

Kylie, based in the opulent comfort of London's St James's Club, favourite haunt of Hollywood superstars like Clint Eastwood, was everywhere it seemed that

summer – and the record sales reflected it around the world. By the end of the year she was rewriting the record books as – with her UK sales alone more than 2 million – she became the first female artist to have her first five singles go silver. Around the world – in Japan where 'I Should Be So Lucky' won record of the year in its top music awards, in Israel where Kylie was voted most popular female singer of the year and Finland where she became the first artist ever to have four consecutive number ones in a year – the picture was the same: gold, silver and platinum framed.

As she entered the most dynamic period of her career, Kylie took stock of the success – and tried to analyse the curious chemistry of the TV series that set her on the road to it.

"At the moment I am just flowing with the tide, following whatever is on offer to me that I like. There is obviously an ambitious streak in me but I do realise that I am still very young and inexperienced. I have never written a song or acted in theatre or a big movie, so there is still lots to learn," she said in her St James's Club suite.

"I realise the market for what I do is very fickle and it could all come to a stop tomorrow. It has already become fashionable to knock Kylie Minogue but I can take it," she added.

"As for *Neighbours* there is always the possibility I could go back to it, the door has been left open for Charlene to reappear at any time.

"I like everyone on the crew and the cast have been amazed at the reaction to it and the way that people have tried to analyse it. But there is no way I would support those who degrade it.

"Soaps like *Neighbours* are pure enter-

tainment and there is nothing wrong with that.

"What appeals to people is the normality of the show, there is nothing do or die about it which makes it very easy to relate to it. *Neighbours* projects being honest and everything has a happy ending. I think the reason the British like it so much is for one thing it is normally sunny, there are some shots outside when it is rainy and overcast, but it comes across as bright and cheerful and it is an ideal sort of world. We are not in an ideal world and so I guess it is like a fantasy to them.

"When they get home at 5.45 they can switch off, they don't even have to think to watch *Neighbours*. Everything is spelt out to them, it is like getting it on a silver platter, so they can go off into another world for half an hour and get lost in this pretend world," said Kylie.

"I owe a hell of a lot to *Neighbours* and I will always remember that. OK so it isn't 'Gone With The Wind,' but it's popular, very popular and I'm proud to have been associated with it . . . "

Ann Charleston and Ian Smith

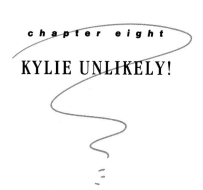

chapter eight

KYLIE UNLIKELY!

"The only thing they didn't say was that I must be pregnant because we were buying a house."

When stories appear along the lines that in another life you were a peasant girl who starved to death during Ireland's potato famine you know you've arrived. Either that or you know that the press has completely run out of lies to write about you. In fact, as Terry Blamey said: "Seventy per cent of everything written about Minogue has been made up."

What is true though, is that the reincarnation tale was one of the tallest stories of them all. According to Melbourne *Sunday Press* reporter Dennis Williams, the paper interviewed a hypnotist, Mr Bill Bakha, who claimed to have taken Kylie back to a former life as a waif called Caitrin in 19th century Ireland. Under hypnosis Kylie was supposed to have said, "It's so cold, cold. I'm in pain. Help me. We are hungry. We are dying. My parents will have to send me away." (A spiteful Sydney paper had added: "What a shame the event went unrecorded. This sounds like her best acting performance in years.")

A session with Bakha was said to have taken place while Kylie was working on *Neighbours*. To add insult to injury the hypnotist claimed Kylie had failed to pay the consultation bill.

Though she laughed at the story and denied it completely, reporter Williams claimed to have a hypnotist's receipt signed by Kylie. The fact that any receipt would have been signed by the hypnotist and not Kylie seemed to have conveniently escaped the zealous Williams.

"And if I hadn't paid why would there be a receipt anyway," protested Kylie quite logically. "It is," she added, "really strange."

But then so are the numerous other fantasies that have been made up about her. For example, there was the Australian edition of the racy *Sunday Sport* which claimed that Kylie had been mauled by a killer shark while skin diving on the Great Barrier Reef. "As the sexy songbird marvelled at the underwater wildlife, the huge maneater moved in to make a meal of the talented star," reported the *Sport*. No surprise to learn that in the same edition the paper ran equally unlikely tales under the headlines, Giant Sprout From Outer Space Ate My Pal and Flying Crocodile Savages Two Kids.

Other stories which have appeared about Kylie seem far more credible. But nonetheless they are lies too. One such story followed one of Australia's prestigious Logie Award ceremonies at which Kylie was a celebrity guest. Australian DJ Brian White told his listeners that a drunken journalist had approached Kylie after she had been presented with an award and asked her if she felt ashamed to have won it in a room full of so many talented people. Kylie was supposed to have burst into tears at the table. No-one else, including Kylie, had any recollection of the encounter.

Similarly another story involved Kylie in an Australian restaurant. "I was supposed to have eaten only half my meal," Kylie remembered. "Someone was supposed to have come up to me and said, 'Didn't you know that there are many starving people in Ethiopia?' to which I'm supposed to have said, 'Yeah. Name two of them'. It didn't happen."

If Kylie didn't know how desperate the press is to write something about her, she might believe she had a double. Someone doing all the things she is alleged to have done.

At one time for example she was reported to have been racing around Melbourne in a brand new pink sports car. At the time she in fact owned and drove a one-year-old red Laser. "At least they almost got the colour right," she says. For a press which had almost always got it completely wrong, this was indeed progress.

At other times they claimed that Kylie had negotiated a one million dollar contract to return to *Neighbours* – a story which Kylie described as wildly untrue. "These reports are a load of rubbish," she said at the time. "The fact is there have been no negotiations for my return to *Neighbours* and there won't be any, at least until I'm back from touring overseas. I'm leaving the show with an open ended ticket," she added.

But no sooner had Kylie mentioned the word overseas than the press began to report that she was about to emigrate from Australia to live in the United States. Again untrue. "A little girl came up to me and said, 'Oh . . . Is it true you're moving to America'. I don't know how the story started, but the truth is I am too close to my family to move away."

On the home front there are also the tales that Kylie was buying a house with Jason Donovan in the inner Melbourne suburb of Richmond. Final proof, the paper said, that the two were "an item". It was true that the two had attended a house auction, but Kylie had simply gone along as a friend while Jason bid for the house he wanted to buy for himself. "The only thing they didn't say was that I must be pregnant because we were buying a house," Kylie joked.

Not so funny, however, were the more hurtful allegations that Kylie was having an affair with rock star Greedy Smith from the Australian group Mental As Anything. "The English press wrote this stuff about us and it nearly broke up his marriage," he said. "The truth is that I had never even met him." At one point the lies had begun to hurt so much that Terry Blamey ordered a total ban on press interviews. "Terry and I tried to cut back on the silly stories by not doing anything at all, but then they attacked the fact that we weren't doing anything," she said.

The lies, of course, continued, only this time instead of light hearted "Kylie Is A Creature From Outer Space" headlines, the press struck straight at Kylie's heart. One target was her mum Carol – now accused of being the archetypal show business

"I can't always ignore what they say but I can say it's a lot of crap."

mother who had pushed both Kylie and Dannii into the limelight. "In fact," countered Kylie, "my parents definitely aren't the pushy showbiz kind. They are happy to see me doing well, but they would never force me into anything I didn't want to do."

Despite this, however, one British magazine went as far as accusing Carol of turning Kylie into an anorexic. A psychologist gave an assessment of the mother/daughter relationship thus: "The classic anorexia symptoms are sometimes inherited and, as Kylie's mother was a ballerina, she would have been weight obsessed all her life. A mother who has put her daughter on the stage and made her into a teenage star is obviously aware that she is moulding something special. She knows there is nothing that is more attractive than the promise of sexuality waiting to bloom, and so if this is what is responsible for fame, Kylie wants to keep her pre-puberty looks."

The press took it as read that Kylie was indeed an anorexic – again something that she has always denied. But at one time the story gained such currency that fans were sending pizzas and Chinese meals to Kylie's Melbourne home. The story actually started when Kylie admitted that she had lost weight after joining *Neighbours* because of the gruelling schedules that the series demanded. And they grew when she told in another interview how she could live on prawns, salad and water, and found eating "a drag".

The fact that she was known to be on a special complex carbohydrate diet designed to help her regain weight didn't help matters. "Other people try to lose weight whereas I'm always trying to gain it," said Kylie. "But that doesn't make me an anorexic. A reporter once called and said, 'Hi Kylie – I hear you're an anorexic'. When the call came I was just about to bite into this huge triple layer sandwich. We all thought that was pretty funny."

Kylie has managed to maintain her sense of humour because she more than anyone understands that in her business it is better to be written about than to be ignored. "The press is also your means to success," she admitted. And as to the over-imaginative way in which papers have so often treated her, she added simply: "Because I'm only young, and have lived such a short and normal life, they run out of things to say about me."

Another theory comes from the serious Australian Magazine journalist Frank Robson. "The attitude seems to be that as Minogue was 'invented' by the publicity machine anyway, she's fair game, no matter how flimsy or outrageous the angle. As a result some publications no longer deal in real information at all, except occasionally by accident."

There is the last and as far as Kylie is concerned most convincing theory, that the stories are the product of small minded, talentless types who can never achieve fame in their own right. "They are fat and ugly and going bald," she said. "They've got nowhere to go in life and they look at someone like me who has sort of got the world at her feet and they are probably as jealous as hell."

Out of all the lies comes one great and simple truth. "I can't always ignore what they write," said Kylie. "But I can say it's a lot of crap!"

chapter nine

THREE INTO ONE DOES GO

Kylie – one of the world's most travelled 21-year-olds – has kept secret a phobia which has always haunted her.

She is terrified of flying . . . so much so that often she has to fight an inner turmoil even to step on the plane.

The feeling of foreboding builds as soon as she wakes and remembers that in a few hours she will be jetting off to yet another exotic location.

It is a major handicap for thousands of people, but for a major star for whom flying is a way of life, it is a living nightmare.

"I would rather do anything than have to fly," says Kylie. "It scares me to death. I just look at the aircraft and wonder 'Is this one going to stay up there'.

"It is something I have had to come to terms with because in the past couple of years I have had to fly hundreds of times. It never gets any better, and I never do any less flying."

Kylie hardly drinks, her occasional tipple is a pina colada, so that is not something she can resort to in order to overcome her nerves.

Instead she has developed a strict routine for short haul trips to get her across her pain barrier.

She explains: "I take a very deep breath before I get on the plane and then as soon as I am on board I get out all my make-up and put it on the table in front of me and spend hours putting it on.

"I usually travel with an assistant from my management company and she does the same so we look a fine pair, both of us sitting there with dozens of jars in front of us, but it does the trick; it takes my mind off the fact that we are 30,000 feet in the air at the time.

"I just don't understand how planes work or what keeps them up there. I don't know why I'm so scared. I suppose because one is so helpless, there's nothing you can do if anything goes wrong and it's an awful long way down.

"I think all the businessmen sitting around me must think I am mad. But it is my way of getting out of a sticky situation. I also find flying so boring, just sitting there for hours."

Kylie is speaking after an amazing journey which tested her nerves to the full. In twenty-four hours she has been on a whistle-stop tour of three countries. Made possible only by the miracle of airborne travel.

"Yesterday I had breakfast in Sweden, lunch in Denmark and dinner in England. If you had told me about that when I was a child, I wouldn't have believed you.

"Travelling is a strange thing. It's a thing I love and hate at the same time. I love it because it means I get to lots of other countries and see different people and different cultures, and I hate it because it is such a hassle and keeps me away from my family and friends.

"Sometimes it does get me down, but I get over that and then it is off to the next place."

Although she spends most of her time in transit between one engagement and another, on arrival the destination often looks pretty like the place she has just left.

The same autograph-hunting crowds wait for her and the same bland interviewers are at hand to ask the same repetitive questions for TV, radio, newspaper or magazines.

"It can be quite samey," says Kylie. "But that's my job. After all it's my choice and I love my career, I'm very lucky."

"I would rather do anything than have to fly."

THE SENSIBLE SUPERSTAR

Above, Kylie is pictured in a West German park.

London in July, 1988, and the showbusiness phrase of the summer is "the Kylie phenomenon". The girl who two years ago was earning $150 a week playing Charlene on *Neighbours* is now the hottest pop property on the planet, commanding £10,000 for the briefest of public appearances and well on her way to selling £24 million worth of records that year.

In the UK alone her fan club has 25,000 members, her début single 'I Should Be So Lucky' has now reached number one in eighteen countries around the world. Her innocent, girlish features seem to stare out of every news-stand in the world.

All around her record executives, film and TV bosses and the media are exhausting their supplies of superlatives. Yet the 20-year-old at the centre of the histrionic hype is impervious to it all. Kylie is cool and she is in control.

She is in no mood to lose all she has achieved since winning that first TV role in *The Sullivans*, nine years ago.

And that means learning much more about the business she is in – most of all, learning to say "no".

Kylie is sitting in a luxurious, £500-a-night suite at the swish St James's Club near London's Pall Mall as she explains she will not be railroaded.

"The important thing for me at the moment is to stay in control. There are pressures building up for me to do all sorts of things but I don't want to accept them," she says confidently, her blue eyes filled with a new purpose.

It is only four weeks since she made her emotional farewell from *Neighbours*, but the self-confident, aware young businesswoman on display bears not the slightest resemblance to the hot-headed, tomboy Charlene Mitchell.

Advised by her accountant father and the increasingly influential Terry Blamey, Kylie is mapping out a career path that will ensure that she is no here-today-gone-tomorrow pop package. Madonna openly boasted of her ten year plan, now Kylie was drawing up hers.

"I don't know if I want be doing this in ten years' time but I certainly believe it is important to plan ahead.

"The other vital thing for me is that I keep on learning. I know I can improve on my acting by taking on more demanding roles, performances that are more difficult than playing Charlene day in day out. There are so many avenues I want to explore in that respect.

"But the day you stop learning is the day you stop altogether," she says.

Among the lessons she is learning is how to monitor the growth of her by now global

"*The day you stop learning is the day you stop altogether.*"

entertainment profile. "When it comes to business I think it is important to get your head down and deal with the accountants and lawyers," she says.

By now, however, the biggest pressure Kylie is facing is for her to move towards live appearances and a major world tour to capitalise on the success of 'I Should Be So Lucky' and all that has followed it. She is adamant that she will not tour until she feels she is ready.

"I don't think that is the right thing for me just at the moment. The idea excites me but it scares me too," she confesses.

She admits there is a competitive streak in Kylie Minogue that is driving her towards live shows simply to silence the knockers. The jibes that she is simply Rick Astley speeded up and has no voice of her own hurt, she says.

"But I know I must not let those people get to me. I know they are saying 'she can't sing' but the important thing to me is that I know I can.

"I sang live on Australian TV just a couple of weeks ago. Everyone was really surprised," she says defiantly. "I think it shut a lot of people up.

"But there is no way I'm going to go on a tour just now simply to grovel to those people who still don't think I can sing."

Kylie's by now worldwide appeal was also bringing overtures from companies desperate for her to endorse their products. This was partly due to 'The Loco-Motion', remixed by Stock, Aitken and Waterman and her third single on the PWL label, succeeding in breaking her in the all-important American market when it climbed to number three in the US charts.

"I am resisting that at the moment. There have been offers from cosmetics and hair product firms for me to do advertising but I have turned them down. I have not done any advertising yet. I am concentrating on music and developing my acting. I really do believe it should be one step at a time," she reveals.

She applies the same, common sense philosophy to the music – despite those who regard her Stock, Aitken and Waterman produced records as mass-produced and moronic.

"I'm aware that you can't move too fast because of your audience. A lot of people have made that mistake and the kids think 'Hang on a minute, we're just beginning to like that stuff', then you change to something completely different. I'm trying to make a gradual move from being Charlene from next door to being Kylie.

"I want to be who I am."

That instinctive understanding of her place in the showbusiness scheme of things was later to rub off on Kylie's fellow *Neighbours* exile Jason Donovan, who was persuaded by his long time friend to abandon ideas of hardening up his dance music into something U2ish. But for now Kylie harnessed it to press on with the next stage of her ten year plan which had been drawn up by her musical gurus. Stock, Aitken and Waterman launched a two month promotional tour of the world in London with a glittering party. The champagne reception – at which Kylie began to demonstrate for the first time a new found confidence with both press and public – also gave them the perfect opportunity to milk their golden child's latest achievement,

three UK gold discs for 'Kylie' the LP, and the singles 'I Should Be So Lucky' and 'Got To Be Certain'.

From there she went on a punishing schedule of visits to the US, Scandinavia and Japan before returning to Australia, which still remains very much her home.

"I suppose there might be a day when I would move away from Australia as my permanent base," she said. "But at the moment whenever I go back to Melbourne after being abroad it seems homelier every time.

"I'm still very close to my family," she said before she embarked on the tour.

"It's all very exciting for me at the moment, here I am about to go around the world for the first time, seeing cities like New York, which I have always dreamed of seeing. I do still have to pinch myself every now and again to convince myself it is really happening . . ."

NEVER WERE THERE MORE DEVOTED SISTERS?

A sister can be a girl's best friend – and sometimes her biggest rival. Kylie and sister Danielle would have their fans believe that they couldn't be closer and that any hint of rivalry is all in the imagination of the press. But the competition which has always existed between them is undeniable.

From their earliest days they were battling it out – sometimes for the same parts. When Dannii (as she likes to be known) was seven she first learned what it was like to lose out to the star quality of her sister. Kylie tagged along when mum Carol took Dannii to the audition for a small part in the soap opera *The Sullivans*. Kylie was spotted by casting director Alan Hardy and snatched the role of Carla, the little Dutch girl, from under Dannii's nose.

"Someone once wrote an awful interview about how I was jealous because Kylie stole that first role from me," Dannii says. "But it wasn't like that at all. They wanted me for the part because it seemed they wanted someone younger. But mum brought Kylie along to the audition as well . . . and she happened to get it."

Later in the girls' see-sawing search for stardom it was Dannii who gained the upper

hand when she landed the plum job singing and dancing in Australia's mega popular *Young Talent Time*. Then it was Kylie who was always introduced as Dannii's sister. "I didn't like it," she recalls. "But I didn't hold it against her in any way."

The sisters were competing again, before the same casting director Alan Hardy, amongst 500 girls trying for the part of Char, the down to earth tearaway in *The Henderson Kids*.

Dannii was the famous sister but Hardy yet again decided to go for the older girl.

He said: "Kylie had prepared really well for the part of Char. She came dressed just like the character. Adult actors do that, but for a kid to

"I'm louder than Kylie. She's really quiet and she's so shy with people."

think of it was terrific.

"She was really bubbly and we knew that we had got the right girl. Because Dannii was famous and they were at the same school, Kylie wanted to make a name for herself. She had spurred on what her sister had achieved."

But *The Henderson Kids* role did not last very long and Dannii still remained the more famous in the Minogue celebrity stakes. Then along came THAT role.

When Kylie finally won her biggest break as Charlene in *Neighbours* she remained modest and unaware that the role would take her to international stardom. "Being known as Danielle's sister doesn't worry me," she told Australian reporters. "But I'm glad to finally be establishing my own identity."

Three years later the tables had turned once more and now Dannii was being asked for interviews in Britain simply because of her sister's fame. Even though back home in Oz she was doing very nicely in the celebrity stakes with *Young Talent Time* and a part in the soap *Home And Away* (which was eventually to follow *Neighbours* as an export to the UK), in the rest of the world she was virtually unheard of.

In a revealing interview with *Woman* magazine it was Dannii's turn to put the record straight. "Everyone would say I am trying to cash in on Kylie," she said "But I'm not.

"We're two different people who happen to be in the same business. I just want to stay in work enjoying what I do. I wouldn't say my career will go the same way as Kylie's – we're both doing our own thing and I wouldn't try to imitate her because we are both completely different.

"I'm louder than Kylie. She's really quiet, and she's so shy with people. I like energetic things, like swimming. She's quieter, she enjoys sewing, things like that."

In other words Dannii had no desire to be packaged as Kylie Mark 2.

This was despite the fact that she too is now branching into her own recording career. "We share a love of singing and music," she says. "But I'm not trying to compete with her."

To prove not just a mutual love of music but a mutual love of each other Kylie and Dannii

sang a duet together at an Australian anti-drugs concert – the song they sang was appropriately called 'Sisters'.

Ironically, at the time both were leading such hectic lives that even though they were both still living at the family home in Melbourne they had almost no time to spend together. Kylie was up at 5am to begin her 12 hour day on the *Neighbours* set while Dannii had her own demanding schedule – combining school studies with her own job on a prime time variety show.

Dannii said at the time: "We don't see a lot of her because our schedules clash really badly. I see her for about ten minutes a week. It's like 'Hi . . . bye' in the door, out of the door. If we are at home at the same time, we are usually both asleep."

Kylie too echoed her sister. "Although we both live at home, we actually don't see much of each other during the week. She's got her work and I've got mine and at night we've only got time to learn our lines before we hit bed."

After Kylie left *Neighbours*, her singing career took off and the international demands on her time were even greater. But for the sisters it meant a chance to get to see more of each other.

As Kylie jetted around the world from one assignment to the next, Dannii took time out from her own hectic schedule to be with her. For five weeks the sisters zoomed around Europe and on to the States. Dannii said: "I had a ball with Kylie."

During the trip the pair were able to indulge in their great shared passion – clothes.

As a youngster Kylie had proved to be a wizard with the needle – amazing friends by being able to run up an outfit in under two hours. One of them, a leather skirt she made for Dannii, still occupies pride of place in her little sister's wardrobe.

An eye for a good outfit is something that both the Minogue girls share. Kylie has been praised for the way she looks – and even made the dress she wore to collect the prestigious Logie TV award in Australia.

She plans to launch her own designer clothes label but that is one area where her younger sister has pipped her at the post. Dannii has already given her name to a range of clothes.

Kylie admits that the tour of the chic boutiques of Paris, London and New York gave the sisters a chance to catch up on a lot of the times they had missed when the demands of television companies just had to take priority over family.

"It was nice just to do shopping and the other sister stuff – in the hours when I wasn't working. These are the things that we have both missed out on over the last few years, both of us working at all times."

The way the Minogue sisters are likely to carry on working, it could be some time before they get the chance of another shopping trip.

A BEACH IN DEVON, ENGLAND

7.45am. 18 August 1989. Exmouth beach on the English Riviera. At such an early hour, the sands of this typically British resort would usually be deserted. On a good day you might happen to come across a man taking his dog for exercise.

Today is different. The locals are already trading gossip about the hundreds of youngsters packing the beach. And Kylie, after two years travelling the world and using England as a base realises for the first time, this really is a home from home. The temperature's hitting the 80's and the kids are wearing day-glo Bermuda shorts and chattering excitedly about the coming day's events.

In another two hours not a grain of sand is visible. 11,000 people are packed onto the shoreline, some of them ankle deep in sea-water. They don't know at the time, but this is to be the biggest event of the unusually hot British summer. DJs are whipping them into a frenzy of anticipation from a stage perched above the masses. The worst-kept secret in the pop world this week has leaked. Kylie Minogue is making a rare live appearance and performance down on the beach. It's school holidays. The word has got round and

Exmouth Beach, Devon, England early on the morning of August 18, 1989 and guess who is comming to town? Kylie fever has sent the temperature soaring and thousands camp out to catch a glimpse of Kylie when she appears as a guest on DJ Simon Mayo's Radio One Roadshow.

thousands have hitched a lift, taken a train or a bus to this outpost which is determined to bask in its moment of fame.

10.30am and a waif-like girl trudges on stage to explain she's lost her parents and doesn't know what to do. "I'm lost, well and truly lost. Where are my mum and dad?" Hordes of admirers screech that they would be only too willing to take Kylie home and look after her for a while. The tousle-haired blonde in a tiny mustard top, and sawn off denims, gives a big teasing wink, and coyly carries on the act. When the "deception" has gone far enough Radio 1's Simon Mayo introduces her to the crowd and milks the ecstatic applause for the benefit of the listening millions tuned into the national pop radio station taking the Roadshow live. She says "Hello" and then reveals an insight into her nature by taking part in a "Scruples" game. Given the dilemma of whether or not to tell a guy his flies are undone, Kylie admits: "If I really fancied him I would. I would do it in a nice way and then he might remember me and ask me out later." The beach roars its approval. As ever Kylie can do no wrong.

Later, over a cup of coffee backstage, Kylie talks frankly about homesickness and how it had taken her two years to adjust to life in England. Yes, she misses her mum and dad, and she misses the golden stretches of beach more than she has ever let on.

"This is great for me," admits Kylie, "I can't thank those people enough for turning up. I'm usually stuck in London and don't meet the real people. These are the real fans and I need to see them. It's a great beach but it's not like my home beach of Port Philip Bay, in Melbourne, which is a bit messy, but seeing the sea I get a

"My life has changed drastically. It has made me a lot tougher and a lot more businesswise."

great urge to swim in it. But yes, I would rather be at home if I had the choice. Of course I miss it there.

"All my family are back there in Australia. London has come to be my second home, but

it has taken some time to get used to it. London really is my work place. I've been coming here for some time and only now am I relaxed there. For quite a while I was pretty lonely. I worked out of town but didn't do a lot else. Now I'm looking for an apartment to call my own, then I will be able to leave all my bags there and have something to return to. In the past I have had to carry all my stuff with me and that has been a drag. I want somewhere I can call home in London.

"It has taken me all this time to get to the position where I can call people up on the phone and go out to dinner or to the cinema. You have to remember I was only 19 when I first came here and people were expecting me to be totally in control. I think I have reached that point now. I'm much more confident about my ability and I have learned a lot. I can't believe how far I have come in the past couple of years. I was very naïve at the beginning but I learn fast. I think of myself as a pretty good businesswoman now.

"I like to involve myself in everything. I couldn't do that at the start. I just wanted to act.

And then sing. Now I want control of as much as I can cope with. It's very hard to see how far I have come. Just look at all these people here today. They have come because they like my music and I owe them everything. It really freaks me to think that people have travelled from all over Britain to this – even though it was supposed to be secret. Without them I would be nowhere. They buy the records and the video, so on days like this I must come out and see them and say 'Thank you' because I am in their debt. Now I am being besieged by offers of films in Hollywood and other areas. I'm not rushing to go to Hollywood. What I am interested in is good scripts. If they are right then I will consider them. They are pouring in right now. Yes some of them have love scenes which I will do if the script is right. I'm an actress, if it is right I will do it. But of course I am aware that people want me to do lots of things because I am Kylie Minogue."

The sharks are learning fast that Kylie isn't about to be eaten for supper. It has taken her just 24 months to learn the rules. "My life has changed drastically. It has made me a lot tougher and a lot more businesswise. I have just turned 21 and I think at this age I am just starting to grow up anyway. I try to keep my eyes on everything. That's why I have a manager and people to do things for me, because some things I just don't have time to do myself. It has taken me quite a while to be able to do that.

"In Australia you are not supposed to have a cleaner or someone to do things for you, there's not such a class distinction. That's why it has taken me a long time to say 'I do work hard, so I need people to do this kind of stuff'."

she says, "and I hope it won't happen to me. I think it is sad if you just want to be popular for the sake of it. You should be aware it could all end tomorrow. You can't rely on popularity to make you happy. I want to enjoy it while it is here, but I have some aspirations . . . like shops," says Kylie, who yearns to own a string of "green" shops.

"The worst thing about being a star is the loss of your private life and all the travel. But I don't think I have missed out on anything. I'm glad I was a normal school kid. If I've missed anything, I have had lots of other things to make up for it. Most of my friends haven't been outside Australia, let alone been all over the world. For instance, when I was first in Britain, I saw all the sights, I could travel on the tube and no-one recognised me. I went everywhere and no-one knew me at all. That was great. But now I've been here nine times and I can't go sightseeing. I can't even stay in a hotel because people find out where I am and they make life a bit of a pain. So I stay with friends. But now it gets more like home every time I'm here."

These days, if Kylie does get a minute to spare in her demanding schedule, she goes shopping. It is her one great vice. Sometimes she even manages to go for a drink or meal with friends. She explains: "There isn't really much time to rest or socialise, I'm really a workaholic and it is what I am used to now. I'd be this busy whatever I did. But I'm always in two minds. Sometimes I think this is great . . . exactly what I want to do. Other times I think, 'What am I doing this for, I could be sitting at home with my feet up.' But then if I really didn't enjoy it, I wouldn't do it, would I?"

". . . I'm really a workaholic and it is what I am used to now."

After the release of stills from *The Delinquents* movie, she's been likened to sex-icon Marilyn Monroe and it is a comparison that Kylie doesn't wish to deny. She is pleased by the attention and the critical acclaim which already ranks her alongside one of the movie greats. "I do have that platinum, suicide blonde hair in the movie," says Kylie, allowing herself a rare giggle, as the guise drops for a moment. But as she heads into the '90s as one of THE global superstars, she's determined not to lose her foothold on reality.

"I can see how people get carried away,"

JASON: TRUTH, LIES AND DECEPTION

They fell in love on screen. They dated, they rowed and they finally got married. And viewers on both sides of the globe lapped up every sugary second of the dream story-line as the ratings soared.

In the real world outside the *Neighbours* studio there were those who were plotting to turn the simmering Scott and Charlene affair into a true-life romance.

Newspapers and magazine offices in Britain and Australia turned their fertile imaginations to the problem in hand. "They must be doing it off screen," insisted hardened news editors.

As with viewing figures, the newsmen knew a juicy liaison, especially if those involved are trying to keep it a secret, does wonders for sales and circulation.

The Kylie and Jason myth was just beginning to grow, and the "love-birds" themselves didn't exactly mind the attention. They and their publicity men realised acres of news space dedicated to the couple would promote not only the TV series but also their own newspapers, and photographers trailed the two stars everywhere during 1988, at the height of the show's popularity.

The success of the series and the regular column inches went hand in hand, as did Kylie and Jason. Pop concerts, film premières and dinner dates. The couple seemed inseparable.

They gave interviews in tandem, coolly maintaining the drama and mystique surrounding the sexy side of the boy and girl next door. On TV stations around the world, they coyly nudged and giggled to each other.

They certainly seemed very much in love.

And then came the bombshell. Pictures were flashed around the world of the two of them cavorting recklessly on a beach.

According to some reports it was Bali, according to others it was Hawaii, but it didn't really matter where. What DID matter was that Kylie, little sweet innocent Charlene, was TOPLESS.

The pictures were rapidly transmitted around the world. An eager public lapped up the vital evidence.

No-one after all would believe Kylie, of all people, would shed her bikini top in the presence of the blond bombshell and frolic in the waves, unless they were an "item." It appeared the world had the evidence it had so long been seeking.

The banner headlines screamed as they splashed the fuzzy, long lens pictures across the newspaper pages.

If it was a turning point in terms of "proving" the relationship, it also marked the change in image Kylie had been wanting for such a long time.

Mummy and Daddy back in Melbourne wouldn't be delighted, but Kylie was unrepentant when she eventually surfaced. Smiling broadly, and displaying the naughty element of her nature, which had been hidden previously behind the candy-coated exterior, she teased reporters.

She confirmed she had been to Hawaii with the hunk and said: "We all had a laugh, that's all. We wanted to go away together and I desperately needed a rest.

"I confess I got a bit of a shock when the pictures appeared. But I'm not ashamed of my body. I like sunbathing topless."

It was a dream interview for the down-market tabloids. Not only proud to display her naked breasts – which attracted some criticism from some quarters for their shape and size – Kylie was revelling in the debate about her body.

Some said she was obsessed with her weight and determined to keep it down to under six stone. This was obviously the way Jason liked it.

"I don't feel good when I think I look heavy," said Kylie. "But I wish people would stop saying I'm anorexic. I am not. I'm just skinny. I survive on fruit, prawns and water. That's enough for me. But I know my fans are concerned. They keep sending takeaway meals to my parents' home to fatten me up.

"Personally I would like to be taller, but certainly not curvier. I don't find a figure like Dolly Parton's attractive. I prefer to be thin.

"I know I am a pin-up to lots of people, but I don't consider myself pretty. I have never been happy with the way I look. You should see me first thing in the morning."

Millions would have loved to have taken her up on her offer. And most were convinced that if there was any one person who could testify to what the pop goddess looked like on waking up, it would be Jason.

But as the romance continued to drag on, there were signs the story was wearing thin, especially for Jason, who was beginning to tire of the façade.

As he began to profess they were "really just good friends", Kylie was strangely sticking to her guns.

Perhaps it was newspaper speculation that the "courting couple" were about to get married that convinced Jason it was time to turn the tide in favour of something nearer the truth and gently let everyone into their secret that it was just one big publicity stunt which, once started, was easier to carry on with than deny, and far more profitable in any event.

And by now, the tabloid writers were switching their attention to other male members of the *Neighbours* cast, and hinting Kylie may be dating them too.

She had already left the show, but the rumours persisted that she was very fond of handsome Aussie stars Alan Dale and Ian Smith.

On them, Kylie was quick to respond and unequivocal with her replies. She admitted that Alan, who played Jason's widowed father, and Ian, who appeared as her own step-father, were very close, but in a simply platonic way. "Ian and Alan are just good friends and I miss them equally as much now I'm away from the show.

"Now that I don't see much of Ian there's no one to call me Floss anymore. He gave me that nickname because I'm small with curly hair like a candyfloss stick, and it's kind of cute.

"He's a really big man, both physically and in terms of his character, and I really looked up to him as a tower of strength when we were doing *Neighbours*."

She revealed it was Alan who took her under his wing when she first joined the cast as a relatively inexperienced actress. She'd done some TV before, but she'd just left school, and had little knowledge of the working world and MEN.

"He likes all women," Kylie giggled as she recalled his masculine effect on her and the other girls in the show.

She added: "When people are sitting around talking about something, Alan will charge off and take immediate action. He's known as a bit of a trouble-maker but he's really helping and striving to make things work well. He is a really nice guy."

Kylie said she got on better with men than women, but put that down to the fact that the three guys in question were the ones she most closely worked with on the series.

The Kylie and Jason "Are they or aren't they in love?" riddle reached its most bewildering moment in September 1988 when she claimed in a woman's magazine that . . . "It's quite true he's my boyfriend and our relationship is very special," while he countered: "It's just not true that we're going out together, or that she's my girlfriend."

The newspapers loved it. This was just like real-life after all. The happy couple warring in public, being at odds over what really was the truth. The cracks in the relationship were starting to show . . .

rumours we have to be careful. We met in London briefly earlier this year and had to make sure we weren't seen in public together." Kylie did agree with him on that.

She confirmed that when seeing each other they always tried to use separate entrances and exits. Suggesting to some, they were already acting like a married couple. It seemed that Jason was keen to distance himself from the increasing danger of being known as the future Mr Minogue.

On screen they had achieved the desired separation. After marrying in the series Charlene ran away to Brisbane "to find herself."

Kylie had quit to further her career in pop, and to look for meatier projects in which to star. It all suited Jason just fine.

"People just like the idea of us being in love," he sighed at the thought of going over ground yet again as he explained the need for him to step out of Kylie's tiny shadow.

"It neatly compartmentalises us, but it is just not true."

"They always photograph me with Kylie because she's my wife on screen, but they never bother to photograph me with other girls. Perhaps they will now."

But then again, not really, if they hadn't been THAT close all along anyway. Jason, always the nice guy, didn't want to upset anybody. Not the papers or the magazines and certainly not Kylie. He did his best to paper over the cracks.

He held his hands up and proclaimed: "I don't want to get into a big row over this and therefore I won't offend *Womans Own* and say they're wrong.

"But the fact is I see Kylie as a best friend and not a lover. I really enjoy her company and miss the fun we used to have together on *Neighbours*.

"But she just isn't my girlfriend. There's no-one in my life right now." Jason was quite firm that marriage was the last thing he wanted.

During a break from filming the successful Australian-made war mini-series *Heroes* in the outback, he said: "I don't have anyone special in my life right now. For one thing there just isn't time. And I know I haven't yet met the right person. It doesn't make me unusual in any way. A lot of people of my age don't want to settle down at this stage."

Movingly he admitted that the divorce of his own parents – actor Terence Donovan and children's TV presenter Sue McIntosh had left deep scars.

Nevertheless he was fond of Kylie and still wanted to have an evening out if they could manage it despite the attention of the ever-present photographers. "Because of all the

He wanted not only an on-screen separation, but one off to match. "I want to get out of that. I'm concentrating on what I'm doing at the moment. When we are so closely associated it becomes a bit of a thing, the two of us together. I'm glad we are going in different directions. I want to filter out all that Kylie and Jason stuff."

Rubbing out Kylie meant, of course, that he could escort other women, without being accused of being unfaithful. "I don't have any problems meeting new girls. I still have time for girlfriends. The funny thing is that people just haven't noticed yet. They always photograph me with Kylie because she's my wife on screen, but they never bother to photograph me with any other girls. Perhaps they might now."

THE PRICE OF FAME

In the two short years that followed her first record Kylie became one of the entertainment phenomena of the 1980s. In 1988 alone she sold a remarkable £25 million worth of records around the world, earning herself around £5 million.

She was garnering awards from Japan to Israel and Ireland, embarking on a movie career that seemed certain to lead to Hollywood stardom – she had even achieved the final confirmation of her status as a member of the élite band entitled to call themselves superstars, a wax image of herself at Madame Tussaud's.

Yet as her Five Star lifestyle moved further and further away from the modest suburban existence of Surrey Hills, Melbourne, Kylie was also learning another lesson.

She was discovering that there was truth in one of showbusiness's most hackneyed old sayings: Fame costs.

There were so many among her High School and *Neighbours* friends who were amazed at the way the shy, fragile, far from self-confident Kylie coped with her instant elevation to international celebrity.

It seemed incongruous to them that the sweet teenager they knew was not only surviving life in

the toughest of all trades, but that she was also winning something of a reputation as a tough cookie, a determined career girl refusing to be deflected from her dreams.

When, in 1988, soon after she had left *Neighbours* to devote herself full time to her music, the cookie looked like it was beginning to crumble, many shook their heads knowingly.

The biggest crisis in her until then trouble-free career came during a recording session in her home town. It was as if, all of a sudden, all the hidden anxieties and fears she had hidden so expertly were now overwhelming her. Kylie ran sobbing out of the studios and did what was still the most natural thing in the world for a 20-year-old girl – she ran home to mummy.

"I was so sick, I had to take a day off. It gave me a few minutes to stop and think about what the hell I was doing.

"I felt . . . What am I doing here? I would rather have a little shop, a holiday home and be getting married and having kids. "There was just so much pressure from so many different people. I just had to say 'Stop'. I had everything, but I had nothing. It's true what they say about that. I am the sort of person, I would like to be a bus driver, work in a nursery. I would like to do everything," she said.

Her near nervous breakdown, which took her to the brink of giving up all she had worked for in showbusiness, was all the more surprising to outsiders given it happened in her native Australia.

Yet it was her own countrymen who first demonstrated the "tall poppy syndrome" she had herself foretold.

The "Singing Budgie" and "We Hate Kylie"

campaign had at first seemed impotent against the simple, unquenchable ambition of Kylie. But she admitted it eventually broke through her defences.

She confessed that the bitter jibes and over-exposure led her to the precipice. "They called me things like plastic person and a bimbo. I am not stupid. If I was stupid I don't think I would have got this far.

"I was sick of seeing myself on television, so I thought the poor public, how are they going to cope. It's over-kill. That's when the public turned against me. But I was contracted. I couldn't stop. I had to keep going."

Asked during those dark days whether she had ever felt like quitting showbusiness she replied; "I would have loved to, but I couldn't."

It is an indication of how low Kylie's emotional defences were during this crisis that – just for once – the intensely personal details of her life suddenly came gushing out, as if to exorcise some spirit that was within her.

She talked of the spectre of Pre Menstrual Tension and how it blighted her life. "I cry, sometimes I am strong and sometimes I burst into tears. Actually I am very emotional. God forbid, when I have PMT you wouldn't want to come near me. I am horrible."

One person who claimed to have witnessed her collapse in the recording studio said: "The poor kid just kept sobbing and saying, 'I can't go on, I can't take the pressure.'

"But the silly girl, just a couple of days later, she was back recording again."

With Kylie at her most vulnerable this was also the time when those who most despised her success happily fuelled rumours that she was anorexic. Reports claimed

that the elfin figured star's weight plunged terrifyingly until she tipped the scales at a mere five stones. They alleged that Kylie confessed, "I honestly thought I was going to fade right away. It was becoming a desperately serious problem.

"At first it was just that, I was too busy to find time to eat. Then I got so that I could not be bothered. And then it got to the stage when I did not want to," she is alleged to have said. "There are always pressures on kids my age to diet and I am no different from the rest.

"But it was turning into a very, very serious problem.

"And only my family saved me. They finally forced me to seek help. When my doctor saw me and heard how much I was working and about the rest of my life, he was absolutely horrified.

"It was stress more than anything that affected me. I could not keep up with the demands of trying to keep everyone happy, and in desperation to make sure I keep my looks,

I gave up eating," she is alleged to have said.

It was claimed that Kylie was placed on a special 1500 calorie a day diet to try to replace the lost weight.

Kylie reportedly admitted in November 1988 that she had the problem back under control.

Talking of the torment she was then emerging from she said: "The demands never end. You are really giving away a part of yourself. You can't even go down the street like anyone else.

"If you are in an office job you can usually go home and leave your job behind. I can't. And you can't get too comfortable with where you are because you could be a nobody tomorrow. When I am tired and think, 'I don't want to do this any more' I just tell myself that it might not be here in a few months and that there's probably a million who would kill to be where I am.

"It is lonely at the top sometimes, most kids my age don't have a care in the world. They can go on the hippy trail up the coast – that's

something I have missed out on.

"I wish I could have done it. A lot of my old school friends are doing that now and they are just hanging loose without a care in the world, it sounds great.

"But there are so many people who want me to do things and I feel I can't let them down. I get home and I have no time to myself. I have to learn things or sign cards for fans.

"If I lived alone I would nearly go crazy. I would feel very lonely. I simply don't get out much to enjoy my success. There is an enormous amount of pressure on me. Sometimes it gets to me, I give so much time and energy to everyone else, that there is nothing left for me.

"That is when I think 'What about me? Am I meant to be the centre of all this?'

"I know I am only 20, but some days I feel about 30 so much has happened to me."

But there was a more sinister side, too.

The rich and famous – and Kylie by now was both – will always be magnets for those disturbed characters like John Lennon's slayer, Mark Chapman; psychotics, infatuated with the darker side of Andy Warhol's chilling message – everyone can be famous for 15 minutes.

From the early days Kylie was plagued by obscene phone calls and hate mail. During her days on *Neighbours*, she recalled how people were only too willing to vent their jealousies publicly.

"Once I was out shopping with a girlfriend and we went into a store. Suddenly a woman just came in, marched up to us, stuck her face in mine and spat '*Neighbours* sucks'.

"Then she turned round, obviously very pleased with herself and walked off. I stood there very amazed but very upset. Why do people do these things?

"Afterwards I told myself 'Who cares what she thinks. If she doesn't like the show she shouldn't watch it'," said Kylie.

The personal abuse continued when Kylie made her base in London. Producer Pete Waterman once had to rescue his starlet from a gang of teenagers when they began spitting at her in a nightclub.

"It is very difficult for me. I remember being pretty shy at school and I think I still am. All the pressures of people having a go at me all the time don't help," said Kylie.

For the media clamouring for every sensational scrap of information about Kylie – good or bad – the troubles she endured during this period were mass circulation manna from heaven.

Even if the stories weren't true.

In October 1988 stories began circulating that Kylie had been the victim of a crazed sex-attacker. It was reported that she disturbed the prowler when she arrived back unexpectedly at her family's Melbourne home. Only a desperate battle with the intruder prevented her becoming the seventh victim of the molester who was then at the top of the Melbourne police 'most wanted' list.

It was claimed that the police investigated the attack which happened as Kylie returned to Australia after another of her visits to Britain. She took a taxi to the family home in Surry Hills and let herself into the house which was unoccupied. She walked into the lounge, the report said, to be confronted with the masked intruder. She began screaming and in desperation threw ornaments and bottles. He made his escape by diving headlong through a porch window.

Kylie, however, vehemently refuses to ever discuss the alleged incident.

Friends within the *Neighbours* cast were said to have claimed the attack left Kylie "badly shaken up."

"She was terrified that the guy had gone looking specifically for her. It is a constant risk for someone like her who is always in the public eye, that someone will develop a fixation on her," the colleague said.

More simple salutary lessons were being learned in Britain too. There, perhaps more than anywhere else, the hunger for tabloid trivia never seemed to satisfy the public.

When Kylie went shopping for more additions to her by now Imelda Marcos scale wardrobe in one of London's stores, the result was inevitable.

'Kylie screams abuse at shop staff' the banner headlines blared.

They insisted she had insulted counter girls after she had been refused discount on a slinky black evening dress which she saw hanging on a rail in the fashionable Hyper Hyper clothes store in London's Kensington High Street.

To other shoppers in the store at the same time such stories were shocking . . .

Top cosmetic company boss Angela Boxer protested: "I don't understand why they were doing this to the poor girl. She did not deserve being pilloried like that at all. I bought the dress she was looking at and chatted to her about it.

"She was polite and didn't make any fuss at all. She was not at all the uppity, self-important celebrity I read about the next day.

"I could not believe the headlines. She was doing her best not to be noticed. Wearing jeans and bomber jacket with no make-up, she wasn't trying to be a big deal at all. I thought she was really very nice and my opinion was formed from that one meeting with her by pure accident. It was not the person I had read about in all the papers and magazines."

But to Kylie the incident was just a re-run of thousands she had lived through before.

She had always accepted the unwritten law of the pop jungle – all publicity is good publicity – and no matter what the excuses, she needed the headlines as much as their writers needed her.

She regularly conceded it was all apart of the 'game' she was involved in. All she needed to do now was put her troubled times behind her and win the game.

Holland Park, London and a private photographic shoot is disrupted when zealous fans find out what is going on. Kylie, said press reports, lost her cool and screamed at the intruders.

I'M A DELINQUENT:
BIG SCREEN DEBUT

When I was fifteen my mother thought I was still a child . . . but that year I discovered life, rock and roll and love with a boy named Brownie Hansen . . ."

Set in Australia in the 1950s, *The Delinquents* celebrates the passionate love story of Lola Lovell, played by Kylie and Brownie Hansen, played by Charlie Schlatter. Brownie and Lola were young and defiant at a time when those who went their own way were considered to be delinquent.

Their parents, the authorities and everyone else thought they were too young to be in love, too young to really cope with adult responsibilities. But together they discover life, rock and roll and love. All their lives they were told they mustn't, they shouldn't, they can't. One year they did! Some rules were meant to be broken.

That's the way Warner Brothers gushingly promoted Kylie's first film.

It's still before dawn on a summer's day in 1989 and the sleek limousine cruises effortlessly along the Pacific Highway towards the Village Roadshow film studios. Kylie's tucked up in the back seat, her mum's alongside, and she's ready to complete the last day's shooting on the £10 million film *The Delinquents*.

As the sun begins to rise she glances out of the window and recalls how she chose this film from all the offers which came pouring in after success on the small screen and on record.

They ranged from the sleazy to the downright soppy. But this was the one Miss Minogue and her handlers gambled upon to turn her into a major star.

Kylie has never disguised her contempt at being sniped at by critics who dismiss her talents as an actress and as a singer.

She still resents being called "The Singing Budgie", the "I Hate Kylie Minogue" T-shirts and Melbourne radio stations who played a song called "I Should Be So Yucky."

Kylie dismisses this with one of her favourite phrases, "It's the Tall Poppy syndrome," she explains. "It is something to do with the way that people want to chop your head off once you get successful."

If she thought she was going to escape the bitching this time round, on the movie, she was mistaken. As ever, there were hurtful reports from "insiders", which portrayed her as argumentative on set. But Kylie wasn't worrying about that right now. She had learned her lines for her final scenes from her sick bed.

If working five days a week on *Neighbours* for two years was tough, her schedule on *Delinquents* really proved it's not all glamour in the movie-making business either.

She and co-star Charlie Schlatter have been toiling flat out for six months. Sweating it out in blistering heat from 6 am until 9 pm each day.

In all that time she only twice took a break from shooting, when she went to Melbourne for her 21st birthday party – a $100,000 family-only blow out at the fashionable Red Eagle Hotel – and a week later for Jason Donovan's birthday bash.

Kylie has felt the pace and has spent the past 24 hours in bed with a stomach upset. She's still looking a little wan.

But the pale complexion will be masked in the make-up room. And as she has shown already, beneath her frail exterior, Kylie is as tough as old boots.

When Kylie first got involved in the film, rock megastar David Bowie was to have been the film's executive producer. She was delighted at having the chance to work with one of the rock world's most distinguished performers who had already branched out into the movie business.

But suddenly David Bowie vanished from the scene, leaving a mystery in his wake.

Some said he quit because he was unhappy at the way the screen play changed the original story.

Written in 1962 by tennis star Pat Cash's late aunt Deirdre Cash, who wrote under the pen-name Criana Rohan, it told the tale of working class urban lovers, who grew up in the harsh environment of Australia in the Fifties.

She died in 1963, years before her critically acclaimed work was being adapted for the silver screen.

Bowie was also supposed to be involved in the score for the film – but eight weeks from its world première in London on Boxing Day, December 26, 1989, distributors Warner Brothers were as confused as those working on the film. A spokesman said: "All we have been told is that orig-inally Bowie was executive producer and then he was supposedly involved in the music.

"Now we are not sure what went on. Bowie had very heavy touring commitments with his new band Tin Machine, and wasn't able to interrupt that."

Warner Brothers said PWL stepped into the breach and were putting together the songs for the movie, including using several old 50's classics by Little Richard, Eddie Cochran and all, while Kylie was doing a cover version of 'Tears On My Pillow', by Little Anthony and the Imperials, and looking for a Christmas Number One.

But she wasn't worried about the way the script finished up and had apparently asked for changes herself.

She told a magazine: "If we'd left it the way it

They don't look much like delinquents on the run. In fact, Kylie and big screen co-star Charlie Schlatter look more like they haven't got a care in the world.

was, it was so depressing you'd have wanted to slash your wrist after seeing it. We've tried to lighten it up."

She played the gutsy Lola Lovell, who got into big trouble with the police and the welfare services after running away with her lover Brownie Hansen, steamily portrayed by Hollywood hunk, Schlatter.

Kylie told the magazine reporter: "I've had a great family life and haven't had the sort of problems she encountered. Lola went through an abortion, moved out of home and was constantly on the run from the cops. I just tried to imagine what it would have felt like, but couldn't draw on any past experiences."

She accepts that if *Delinquents* is the success everyone says it will be, the next logical step will be Hollywood.

After all she has been compared to Monroe, a parallel she doesn't argue with although she insists she won't get into the same mess as the icon who screwed up her life with an overdose of men, booze and drugs.

"I went to Hollywood on a promotional tour in the summer of '88 and it wasn't quite what I expected. I was really disappointed with it I suppose, it just didn't match up to my expectations. I thought many parts of it were pretty drab.

"I'm sure I could get used to it though.

"I get lots of film synopses sent to me and after this movie I hope I will get a lot more. I want a bigger range to choose from and hopefully this role will help me.

"I really do want to do more TV and film work. I want to get more experience under my belt.

"I don't think there is any rush for me to get to America and make films. I don't think it's a

"Lola went through such a lot at a young age – I admire her – I'm certainly not as strong as she is."

big deal. Major movies are being made all the time in other countries, particularly in Australia and Britain, so I'm not in any race to get to Hollywood. I don't think it is the be all and end all. We'll just have to wait and see."

The car pulls up at the studio and Kylie greets everyone with a breezy "G'Day" and gets ready for the last few moments as Lola teenage runaway.

She's cast off Charlene's greasy overalls and pulled on a few slinky numbers for this role. And Charlie, as her lover, bears more than a passing resemblance to yesterday's hero, James Dean.

But as ever the focus is on Kylie.

Lola gets up to no good with her handsome boyfriend, but it's a basic boy meets girl story of how the pair defiantly take on the world.

There are some steamy bed scenes, which may be too hot for most of Kylie's young fans to see, but it could turn a whole new audience on to her charms.

"The whole experience has been a lot of fun and the crew have been fantastic, especially in the very beginning because I was nervous for the first few days. It was, after all, my film début, and you only get one chance at that. I did feel I had to

live up to certain expectations, but even more than that I wanted, for myself, to do the best work that I was capable of."

Kylie tried hard to research the part of the wayward Lola whose life had been so very different from her own. "The role is very powerful, although at the same time Lola is very sensitive. Her character goes through a number of changes which is very interesting. I tried to do research on the 1950s but it was quite hard to find general information about the day-to-day lives of 1950s teenagers.

"She went through a lot that I haven't been through. I think that everyone probably goes through fights with their parents during their early teens but I certainly didn't know what it was like to run away from home and to have constant dealings with the police and welfare organisations. Lola went through such a lot at a young age – I admire her – I'm certainly not as strong as she is."

"I was looking forward to the film because there is a beginning and an end, and I knew where the character was going."

Kylie discovered the enormous difference between acting for television and acting for films. "People had said to me that I'd have a lot of spare time on the film set – oh sure! I also found the work to be a lot more precise and everyone put that little bit of extra effort into their work. With a television series there's just not the time for that, and it can often become very much of a routine. I was looking forward to the film because there's a beginning and an end, and I knew exactly where the character was going. With a television series you never know from one day to another what your character will be doing next, which makes it that much harder."

The crew were more than complimentary about the way Kylie has played the young siren.

She's so convincing that co-producer Alex Cutler promises, "She'll break your heart".

Other interviewers who met her on set have tried to solve the riddle of her success. The mystery of the appeal. What the hell has she got that makes her so special?

One wrote: "Anyone who's seen *Neighbours* knows Kylie's no Glenda Jackson. Her singing sounds alright but there are plenty of kids who could do that after a whirl in Stock, Aitken and

Waterman's mixmaster.

"She's not even particularly beautiful, rather pretty in that perky, timeless girl next door way. So there it is: the Kylie paradox.

"She's so ordinary she's special. She is all things to all people because everyday folk easily identify with her.

"She's the young woman at the bus stop, the check-out girl at the supermarket, the clerk at the building society. Kylie is for every youngster the manifestation of a dream. If she can do it, they can do it. Life holds infinite promises.

"Charlene could have been anyone's sister, anyone's daughter. Most people know someone like her. So when Kylie stepped out of Ramsay Street to try something new, everyone went with her. They wanted her to succeed, just as they would have wanted someone from their own family to make it.

"She was a simple commodity with a squeaky-clean public image and there wasn't, still isn't – a kid who didn't want to be like her or a parent who would discourage their children from admiring her."

And as top Australian journalist Richard Shears sums up in his stylish appraisal of Kylie the phenomenon: "At the end of the year Britons will be able to make up their own minds when *Delinquents* is released. If they don't like it, well, there's always *Neighbours* to go home to . . . "

It is an able assessment which completely tallies with Kylie's own view on her career to date.

She adored working on the million pound project which was predicted would rival Paul Hogan's *Crocodile Dundee* smashes.

"It's been wonderful," she said. "It is just brilliant to get away from the image of Charlene in *Neighbours*.

"I've been offered lots of films just because the producers thought I would put bums on seats. But this one really appealed to me. It is about young love in the 50's and has a universal appeal.

"I don't think I will lose my fans. I may gain more acceptance. People will be able to identify with Lola who is just a child without a family, trying to stay alive and fall in love.

"Lola is very powerful and very sensitive and she goes through a lot of changes. I felt there was something there I could grab hold of, whereas a lot of the scripts that were offered to me before were pretty crummy.

"There were a lot of seductive scenes and that sort of stuff and a lot of characters that were a complete copy of Charlene and I wanted to get away from that."

Kylie was also keen to get away from the mass-produced soap to work with material of a more sophisticated calibre. She was fed up with the factory-style working conditions involved in producing a day-in-day-out series.

She explained: "In a series you never know what is around the corner because the lines develop from episode to episode. Of course it is very hard for the writers because they have to keep things up to date and follow the story-lines.

"They don't get the time to turn out a script of real quality. But that is what I like about this film. The script is of such a high standard. It has got a start and a finish and you know what is going on."

In production the film was expected to be granted an '18' certificate because of its tough screenplay.

Gradually Lola changes from a book-reading teenager in a small town in Fifties Australia. She loses her innocence to a Teddy Boy, switching from gymslip and satchel into Monroe wig and padded bra, in a dramatic saga that culminates in pregnancy, abortion and law-breaking.

A critic who saw the rushes said: "It will probably not be seen by Kylie's younger fans because of its content. But it will prove that Miss Normal Superstar has one great gift: the camera loves her.

"When Hollywood sees her luminescent qualities, they will steal her forever."

The sexual content of the film did give Kylie pause for thought. But after carefully considering the plot and the situation, she accepted the raunchy bits, because she believed they were true to life.

"Realism is important to me. I don't mind the idea of doing love scenes if they are part and parcel of the job and not inserted for sensational reasons.

"I really don't think this film goes over the top in any way. I think it is very moving."

If Kylie is happy with her work, she considers

she's over the main hurdle. But like every artist, one can always look back and see where things could have been improved.

As she said: "I always think there is more to do. And I have got so much more to learn. This is my first film. I've never done theatre; I've never done song-writing; I haven't done much live work, there's a multitude of things to do. I'm interested in things outside of entertainment as well, and although I feel I'm older than 21, I have to remind myself that I am 21 and I've got a lot of years ahead."

She was nervous before stepping onto the set of *Delinquents*, just as she had been all those years ago when she did the rehearsals for *The Henderson Kids*.

"This was my big one, my début. You can't do a début again can you? You only get one chance at it. I think I was a little bit nervous because there are so many expectations of me," she said.

On another part of the movie lot, Charlie Schlatter was learning his final lines of the drama. With his dark and smouldering looks, he was the envy of millions of youngsters because he actually gets to kiss Kylie, and a little bit more too.

According to reports in some of the more scurrilous publications, the young American was deeply turned off by this close encounter with the "world's sexist female" as Kylie has been voted in many teen surveys.

They claimed that before the cameras began to roll Kylie and Charlie could be seen locked in heated discussion about just how heavy they should get in the love scene.

Apparently Kylie was usually the one to surrender to Charlie's heavyweight protestations. After all SHE was the newcomer, and HE had starred alongside Michael J Fox in *Bright Lights, Big City*, and was better known in the movie-world.

They were kissing each other through gritted teeth, so the story went.

And Charlie was alleged to have told reporters: "It was hardly a turn-on."

The producers wanted to ensure the film was a hit in the States, they too were happy for Charlie to call the shots.

One on-set photographer was quoted as saying: "It became a standing joke that Kylie could be heard saying: 'Charlie's right'."

But back to Charlie and those gossipy tales about the steamy scenes that had been filmed behind closed doors: "There's no running around naked – it's not a porno film. It's pretty tasteful and although you do see me naked, it is done from a distance," she said.

That was a defence she would have to repeat – again and again.

I SHOULD BE SO MUCKY

I n Ramsay Street the transformation would have set tittle-tattling tongues working overtime for months. Suddenly the little girl lost, the lovable teenager, had gone through a startling catharsis. Here was Kylie, the tomboyish Charlene, provocatively posing in brocade bodices, glitzy mini-skirts and shorts – revealing nigh – or is it thigh – on all to the world.

The emergence of the New Kylie came in the autumn of 1989. In the build up to her first ever world tour, the now seasoned campaigner decided it was time to kill the cutesy girl-next-door and reflect the reality of what had happened to her over the previous two years.

So out went the playful jean and mechanic's dungarees and in came haute couture, designer wear from around the world she was about to begin a campaign to conquer. Image - an ever present ingredient in the alchemy of pop – was now reflecting Kylie's transformation from naïve to knowing superstar.

The only confusion was deliberately manufactured – was she now a Lady or a Vamp.

With work on her first feature film *The Delinquents* behind her and a new collection of singles successfully launched with 'Hand On Your Heart' topping charts all over the globe,

Kylie herself was busy adding her own mystique to this great debate.

"I suppose I have always seen myself as a younger version of Joan Collins," she confided. "This is the kind of acting part I want to be offered in future. If I get a good script and it calls me to do a hefty love scene why not?" she added, lips that were once sugary and innocent now curled coquettishly.

"I have always seen myself as a younger version of Joan Collins."

Pete Waterman had once promised his prodigy that one day he would transform her into the Madonna. His prophecy was now coming true, perhaps even sooner than he would have dreamed. Less than two years into his master plan Kylie's words already carried the brashness and naked ambition of pop's Queen of Sleaze.

She talked about plans for another mini-series, hinting that those 'hefty' sex scenes may not be too far away. "I'm considering doing a mini-series set in the 1940s or 50s called *The Silence Of Dean Maitland*. He is a priest and I play a young girl called Diane who he has an affair with. It is very heated and more than anything else I have done would take me a million miles from the safety of Ramsay Street," she said.

Her choice of leading man in this *Thorn Birds*-style shocker revealed much too about the new, confident Kylie. "It would be right in some ways for big stars like Jack Nicholson or William Hurt, but to me they are too old," she said.

Instead she nominated some of the sexiest men in the entertainment world. "The guys I would like to work with would be Mel Gibson or Michael Hutchence from the Australian band INXS. The other actor I really like is River Phoenix," she added.

There were plenty of critics ready to knock the new look girl wonder. The "I Should Be So Yucky" headlines returned as though by becoming more glamorous Kylie was jettisoning the secret of her success – her ordinariness.

But Kylie herself was now in complete control of her own mind and her own career. She was even making her own clothes which she often paraded at public appearances in Britain and Australia.

And if she wasn't making her own clothes, she was determined to back her country folk and wear designer gear from Down Under, not previously known as a stronghold in fashion terms.

But by mid-1989, Kylie was THE figurehead of High Street fashion throughout Europe, which was very good news for Sydney's pauvre couture set, who were beginning to find international recognition at last.

Like Australian rock music, the country's fashion houses had taken several decades to find acceptance and Kylie was keen to do her bit.

"I love the clothes from home. There are so many great young designers there now and everybody knows just how much I love shopping for clothes," said Kylie.

One of the people to mastermind the jeans clad mechanic transformed into a sex symbol was the Sydney fashion guru, Nicole Bonython.

She explained: "I was called in at the last minute to help style a photographic session for Kylie about 18 months ago and it went from there. She liked the clothes I supplied for her and we now collaborate on her wardrobe."

Nicole teams up with Australia's leading contemporary designer, Stephen Galloway, when the star wants sophistication and haute couture.

Galloway, who received the high accolade of the Cointreau award for innovative design, said the choice of what Kylie should wear was left up to Nicole. "Nicole comes into the workrooms, selects the cloths, and Kylie make the decisions and then I make them to order," he said.

But her favourite design team of Peter Morrissey and Leona Edminston, who have their own small shop in Sydney's Strand Arcade, are charged with making her fun outfits.

A display of the couple's clothes was put on show at an exhibition of contemporary Australian fashion at London's Victoria and Albert Museum in 1989.

Kylie's wardrobe bulges with skintight dresses, little lurex numbers, sexy catsuits and even a rafia bra from their collection.

Their main problem is cutting the clothes to fit Kylie's petite size 6 figure.

"She's so little that we re-make everything to her size. She's like a little doll" said Morrissey. "We think it is important that clothing shouldn't overwhelm the wearer, but that a definite sense of a person's character be enhanced and exaggerated. Our clothes should look different on everybody who wears them.

"Currently she's got a lot of our designs in her wardrobe and the last time she was in Australia we had dinner together."

Bizarrely, Kylie turned to the influence of Ned Kelly for inspection. She wanted clothes which reflected the 19th century Australian outlaw's wild and woolly look, and hired the latest member of her design team, Ian McMaugh, to provide it. He is known for his dull, green eucalyptus and bushland colour creations and finely structured suits.

He also provided the satin and sequins image seen on Kylie's Japanese tour, along with pearl bustiers, feathered skirts and tight beaded dresses.

Her love-affairs with clothes suggested yet another career for Kylie. And who knows? We may soon see her own range of fashions.

"... I used to just like comfortable clothes but now I'm more into dressing up."

"I have always thought that I would like to be a fashion designer. There was a time years ago when I made the odd item of clothing and I have started designing stuff again now. I used to just like comfortable clothes but now I'm more into dressing up," she reveals.

With reports in wide circulation that she was amassing a multi-million fortune at the rate of £620,000 a month, Kylie was also able to indulge her passion for shopping.

She became a familiar figure at some of London's top stores, particularly in Kensington High Street, around the corner from the luxury £400,000 Holland Park Flat she shared with her Neighbours/PWL stablemate Jason Donovan. The designer shop Hyper Hyper and the nooks and crannies of the Kensington Market complex were favourite haunts of Kylie's, who often shopped without her minders, dressed simply and in dark glasses for anonymity.

Every acquisition was carefully stored in a massive wardrobe the magpie-like singer was building up. "I hate throwing things out, I am a real hoarder. One day I know I won't have room for everything but for the moment I won't bring myself to part with something I have found," she said.

The new Kylie was also fiercely protective of her image too. In the early days she had been stung by criticism of the way she dressed. One of her first arrivals at Heathrow gave the British tabloids a field day as she climbed off a long-haul flight from Australia in the same travel-weary outfit she had boarded in. The headlines, this time 'I Should Be So Scruffy', ensured she never made the same mistake again. Taking a leaf out of her newest role model Joan Collins' book, Kylie never again emerged through a customs hall before spending as long as was needed to make herself ready for the waiting world.

Her experience during rehearsal for her first Royal Variety Show at the London Palladium in November 1988 also taught her a lesson. Not realising photographers are traditionally allowed in to the run-through Kylie emerged on stage in scruffy jeans. Making matters worse there were slip ups too when she tried miming to a backing tape. When less than a year later she topped the bill with Jason at a Children's Royal Variety show at the Dominion Theatre she was not about to make the same error of judgement. First Kylie emerged for the rehearsal in the same impeccable outfit she was due to wear in front of Princess Margaret that night, and ran through a flawless performance of her then new single 'Hand On Your Heart'.

Then, to rub things in for the assembled paparazzi, Kylie made the photographers sign legal forms as they entered the theatre. The documents signed over all legal rights of the pictures to her. The never-slow-on-the-uptake Miss Minogue was not about to lose control of the carefully constructed image she had worked so hard on and that was a victory which put many a sharp-practising lensman on his guard from then on.

Such was Kylie's hatred of what she called 'pirate' pictures of her that she instructed her lawyers to look into ways of suing those who published unofficial photographs of her on the myriad items of memorabilia that filled shops all over the world. "Kylie feels she should have copyright over her image, that is the way it is in Australia and that is the way she thinks it should be everywhere. She can't believe photographers can get away with so much here," said her manager during that visit to London, Jason's trusted right hand man Richard East.

Such was the confidence of the little girl they used to call 'Shorty' at school that she was now considering taking on the might of the English legal system. The verdict on that one, however, may have to wait for many years yet.

KYLIE – LIVE AND UNLEASHED

.50 pm on an October Sunday afternoon. Two thousand already frenzied teenagers – watched over by an army of protective bodyguards dispensing coke and caring words rather than the customary threats – are now at fever pitch.

They are crammed into the art-deco Le Palais disco in Hammersmith to celebrate the 16th birthday of London's top radio station, Capital. Some of pop's flavour-of-the-month acts are on the bill. Already they have seen the hip-swivelling dance trio The London Boys, comeback-making Curiosity Killed The Cat and the ebullient Sonia, latest perfectly packaged product to roll off the Stock, Aitken and Waterman production line. But now they wait in far-from-quiet anticipation for the main event.

The pre-pubescent shrieks suddenly reach a crescendo as the chugging electronic beat of the opening bars of 'The Locomotion' blasts out of the vast sound system. Pandemonium breaks out as, flanked by a giant blue cut-out wooden train, Kylie steams on stage. This is her first live appearance in Britain – the country responsible more than any other for creating the Kylie phenomenon. It is also a nation waiting for her to fall flat on her face.

From the opening routine, however, it is clear Kylie is not about to play into the hands of those waiting to propel her off her pedestal. Dressed first in a spangled blue bra top and sequined red shorts, she is step perfect. Weeks of painstaking work on the complex choreography of her 40 minute show pay off as she struts, high-kicks and glides around the tiny, tightly guarded stage singing the song that first gave her the confidence to dream of a career as a pop star.

Within minutes that now over-brimming confidence is shining through as brightly as her dazzling stage outfit. The vampish side of the New Kylie comes with it. Her sensual, teasing routine would have been unlikely to get a '15' certificate at a British cinema. The strictly 14 to 18 year-old audience – as well as the older entourage or pressmen and record company executives – are left staring in wonder.

"I thought this was supposed to be the goody, goody girl I live next door to," said one wide-eyed recording chief as he watched Kylie cavort provocatively below him.

The faintly wicked smile now breaking on Kylie's sweat stained face was already warning "You Ain't Seen Nothing Yet".

The tour she had waited so long to unleash had begun two weeks earlier on the other side of the world. Like Michael Jackson, Madonna and George Michael before her, Kylie chose the world's second most important pop market to launch herself on a planet desperate to see her perform. More than 40,000 ecstatic fans filled stadia each night to scream at the girl they instantly dubbed the Mighty Minogue.

And in a series of four concerts she confirmed her status as the number one star in Japan. The success of those appearances in the cities of Tokyo and Nagoya owed everything to the professionalism that had transformed Kylie in two short years from innocent to hard-headed star.

Kylie live on stage during the *The Hit Man* tour of *Britain* in October, 1989. She confounded her critics and confirmed her massive popularity.

No one had been more painfully aware of the importance of her début concerts than Kylie. For more than a year – ever since her début album became a worldwide number one – she had fiercely resisted every pressure to capitalise on her phenomenal record sales with a series of live stage shows. The common sense, suburban philosophy of the accountant's daughter from Surrey Hills – "one thing at a ime," forever ringing in her ear – over-rode all the tempting words Stock, Aitken and Waterman and the money men of pop bombarded her with.

Carefully she waited until the right moment. And when it came its execution was planned with the perfectionist's precision that was already Kylie's hallmark.

Even her guru, Pete Waterman, was not privy to the secret preparations for the opening concerts in Japan and Britain. His increasingly independent protégée locked herself away in a London dance studio for three weeks perfecting what was to be one of the most talked about dance routines of the pop year.

Even Waterman's own trusted experts, stylist Sharron and dancer Clare, both of whom had been a backbone of Kylie's organisation, took a back seat as Kylie took control herself. Only black dancer Venol, who was to share the stage with the star throughout the gruelling tour, was allowed any major influence during those crucial weeks.

"She insisted we didn't see the show before the first night," explained Waterman. "It was a very important step for her, and typically she wanted to be in control of it," he added.

When Waterman finally got a glimpse of the superstar he had created he saw a Kylie unlike anything he had seen before. Yes, the familiar

"It is a pretty daunting prospect going on stage for forty minutes but it does not seem to have fazed her."

compulsive interest in clothes was there for all to see as Kylie unveiled a stunning collection of outfits – some chic and stylish others garish and outrageous. The thriftiness she often boasted of was also in evidence – despite their opulent appearance the costumes cost just £3,000. But what was totally unfamiliar was the athleticism and poised stage presence she had achieved in such a short time. Taking a leaf out of Madonna's book once more, Kylie had punished her tiny body with a strict daily keep fit routine. Dumb bells, hours of exercising and a carefully planned diet of vegetarian food and fruit juice had completed the programme. The end result was Kylie physically equipped for anything touring could demand of her – and an accomplished dancer.

As he watched her début in London, Waterman wore the expression of a father seeing his daughter metamorphosing from girl into woman before his very eyes. "She never ceases to amaze me," he said, Perrier water with lime clutched to his chest as he stood on the balcony above the stage where Kylie was ridding herself forever of her cutesy image.

"She deliberately kept us in the dark because she wanted to prove that she could get over this monster barrier of performing live on her own. What she has achieved is remarkable given she is still very young and has only been in this business a couple of years. It is a pretty daunting prospect going on stage for forty minutes but it does not seem to have fazed her," said the millionaire producer.

In those forty minutes Kylie packed in eight songs and no less than four costume changes. But it was the dynamic sexuality of her act that grabbed the headlines and confirmed her arrival as a new musical siren.

After the high energy opening of 'The Locomotion' Kylie launched herself into a raunchy version of her second big hit 'Got To Be Certain'. Thrusting and grinding around the stage in unison with her dancers, she made the message clear – "I'm no longer safe little Charlene". The vamp was soon turning into a lady again though, and by the third song, a moody version of the classic Little Anthony and the Imperials hit 'Tears On My Pillow', the audience was seeing a sophisticated side of Kylie too. Draped in a red feather boa, she playfully cuddled her quintet of dancers, all of whom were dressed in sailors outfits.

The real sensation came, however, during the fourth number. The mood began elegantly enough. Kylie reappeared on stage in a baggy white zoot suit to sing another of her personal favourites, 'Je Ne Sais Pas Pourquoi'. But as the song blended into 'Made In Heaven' the unthinkable happened. Off came the stylish suit and soon she was again prancing provocatively around the stage in a skimpy pink sequined bra and shorts.

Kylie's sensational striptease act predictably collected most of the headlines next morning in Britain. "Oh Kylie, what will the *Neighbours* say? Mrs Mangle would be mortified, Harold horrified . . . and Scott would go spare. TV's girl next door does a striptease," they screamed. But it also symbolised the latest stage in her development. Kylie had cathartically climbed out of her demure old skin into a naughtier new one – with the world watching.

Such was her determination to break the old mould that she was totally unaffected by the sudden appearance of Curiosity Killed the Cat star Ben Volpeliere-Pierrot on stage midway through one of her routines. The gangly singer – who later admitted he was the worse for wear for drink – ineptly mimicked Kylie and her dancers for two embarrassing minutes. But both Kylie and Waterman ignored the incident, refusing to let it cloud her triumph.

"There is always someone who wants to steal the limelight," Waterman said after the concert. "But Kylie was not at all affected by it," he added.

By the time she left the stage – 'I Should Be So Lucky' was the predictable finale – both he and his most successful star had survived their sternest test. Kylie's voice – backed up by a

sophisticated set of taped effects in case of emergency – had silenced many of her critics. Aretha Franklin she was not – but the myth that her voice was never an ingredient on any of her hits had finally been laid to rest. She had also come through a baptism in front of Britain's most demanding audience.

Taking stock afterwards Waterman – for one – was counting the afternoon as a turning point.

"London was always going to be the most difficult test. Japan had never seen her before and she is now so popular there she could not fail really. But here people are more critical, kids are used to seeing all the big names," he said. "Going out in front of two thousand kids like that was difficult for her and she was very nervous about it. But she has now gone through that barrier and that is important for her."

Relaxing in the bar of Le Palais after the sweat-soaked teenagers had trouped off into a sunny Autumn afternoon, Waterman explained the strategy behind this latest step in Kylie's inexorable rise.

The producer, who was himself about to take the reins of the tour as it moved on to the regions of Britain as the Coca Cola Hit Man roadshow with Sinitta, Sonia and others from his stable below Kylie on the bill, said plans to take her to major stadia like Wembley had been quickly dismissed.

"I would love to have seen 400,000 kids coming along to see Kylie on this tour, but it just is not possible," said Waterman. "We are not ready for big venues like Wembley yet, maybe next time but not now. The important thing with this tour is that it is personal. Kylie wanted to personally say thank you to all the kids who have bought her records and for it to be worthwhile you need to have kids within twenty feet of her. Otherwise they are half a mile away and it is ridiculous. In Japan there were more than 40,000 kids there but they were so far away she must have physically looked half an inch high.

"Here we wanted kids to know that physically Kylie is real. We wanted them to say as they leave 'I have seen Kylie Minogue'. Here they have seen her because they have been within thirty feet of her. We looked at Wembley Arena and the National Exhibition Centre in Birmingham and we said 'no'. We wanted this first tour to give some feeling to the kids."

All tickets for Kylie's ten Coca Cola shows were distributed free through local radio

Kylie's sensational striptease act predictably collected most of the headlines next morning in Britain.

stations. In a typically astute piece of marketing Terry Blamey and PWL saw that – with a major multi- million-pound sponsor behind them – allowing fans in free would further endear Kylie to her record buying public without also eating heavily into profits. The only problem was dealing with the thousands of disappointed fans.

"About 30,000 fans will see her as she travels around the country. We are sorry that she won't be seen by more but it just has not been possible. We decided to give the tickets away through competitions and stuff like that on local radio stations because that way the true fans of her music will get to see her.

"We could have just announced that free tickets were available at the door but after talking to the police about it we decided that was a bad idea. There would have been riots if we had let thousands of kids come along like that," said Waterman.

"This way we will actually lose a lot of money. But as far as we are concerned it is not about money, it is about thanking the fans. Kylie feels that way too and has put a lot of her own money into the tour too."

With only one tenth of her début British tour safely negotiated, however, Waterman was already envisaging more – and bigger – tours for Kylie.

"With Kylie you have to remember this is only the beginning," he said enthusiastically. "This is just a confidence tour in many ways. It is tuition for her and helps her to get over a lot of barriers about performing live in front of demanding and sometimes difficult audiences.

"This tour will make her want to do more, so next year we will hopefully be able to work with a band and do things on a grander scale. As I say this is only the beginning . . ."

From London, Kylie headed west to Swansea in Wales and a tearful reunion with her Welsh relatives. The bond between the Australian and Welsh branches of the Minogue clan had always been strong. Kylie's grandparents Dennis and Millie Jones were fiercely proud of their roots in the valleys and instilled in their family a respect for Welsh tradition and culture. The Jones and Minogue families were prominent figures in Melbourne's Welsh society – the Cymdeithas Cymraeg – joining each March 1st in the St David's Day celebrations and eisteddfods or singing festivals.

And they kept in close contact with the family in Wales. In particular they never forgot Dennis and Joan Riddiford, Millie's brother and sister-in-law whose life together in Australia was cruelly cut short when Dennis contracted malaria. Kylie wrote regularly to the Riddifords and also her great aunt, Dilys Evans, a sprightly 80-year-old who still worked as a waitress in the town of Maesteg. The family loving superstar even organised a secret gathering of the clan in Bath in October 1988, booking Dennis, Joan, Dilys and Dennis's sister and brother-in-law Nancy and David into the luxurious Beaufort Arms Hotel for a night. Amid tight security, Kylie and her mother Carol, along with a posse of security men, took a day off recording to spend a day in the country with her relatives.

A month later Kylie also made sure that Dennis and Joan were in the audience when she appeared before the Queen Mother at the Royal Variety Performance. The generous niece even booked the couple a £200-a-night room at The Dorchester so they could enjoy the show at the famous London Palladium.

So performing live in the Land of Song for the first time was an emotional experience for Kylie and her relatives. Kylie had been a 13-year-old slip of a thing when she had last stayed with Dennis and Joan in their home in the village of Cymmer. The provocative, practised performer they saw on stage that night was a niece to be even more proud ot.

"She is a grown woman now, she has changed a great deal since she last came to stay with us eight years ago," said Mrs Riddiford after meeting Kylie in her hotel after the concert.

"We have seen her a few times since she has become well known. We are a close family and she has always stayed in touch. But because she is so busy we have had to travel to see her, it was nice to get together here in Wales," said Mrs Riddiford.

"We took our three grandchildren along with us, they were very excited about meeting her," she added. "They like her music very much but to be honest I am of the older régime, I prefer the traditional Welsh choral music. "But we are all very proud of what she has done," said Mrs Riddiford.

The only cloud over Kylie's Welsh reunion was the absence of another of her favourite aunts, Mrs Thomas Riddiford. She suffers from arthritis in her hip which keeps her confined to her home in the town of Maesteg. The 85-year-old Mrs Riddiford was left to gaze admiringly at photographs in the Welsh national newspaper *The Western Mail* which was full of Kylie's triumph the morning after. "I would have loved to have been there but I just cannot get around now. I need crutches to get around the house and could not get to the concert," she said.

"But like the rest of the family I am very proud of little Kylie. Joan and Dennis will tell me all about it I'm sure and I expect I will get a Christmas card from Kylie and her mother and father," she added.

Kylie in Bath with her favourite aunts and uncles, David, Joan, Nancy and Dilys

Kylie signing autographs for her aunt Dilys

Kylie kept up a relentless pace during the tour, which took her to Newcastle, Manchester and Liverpool before one appearance in Scotland at Edinburgh's Playhouse Theatre. Despite the way she discreetly booked into hotels as plain Miss Jones, she was ever available for interviews on local radio stations and always willing to pose with winners of concert tickets in the evening papers. She even found time to return to London for appearances on top pop shows where she revealed she was angry about the way under 14s had been excluded from her concerts.

"I'm annoyed about that, it was only when I began touring that I heard about it," she told the BBC's top children's programme *Going Live*. "I'm disappointed for those under 14s who haven't had a chance to see me this time, but I'm looking forward to doing a full scale tour probably next year when everyone will have a chance to come along," she added.

Her performances – and the perfectly packaged promotion that went with it – won Kylie new fans of all ages. Even pensioners turned out, even though like under the 14s they

"It is rather like the older generation's fascination with the Royal Family."

were not allowed in to see the shows.

Les Hipkiss, a sprightly 62-year-old from Birmingham, queued for hours to catch a glimpse of the diminutive star. "I watch her almost every day on *Neighbours*. I admire her because she is an actress who can also sing and I think she has a wonderful personality," said Mr Hipkiss as he stood with 1,500 screaming fans outside the city's Ritzy nightclub.

Her appeal to all generations was now something that separated her from almost any other pop star of her generation. Children yearned to be like her and parents, even grandparents, were happy to see their young modelling themselves on a star seemingly unsullied by the darker side of rock and roll. "Kylie's not a threat, she is considerate and not into drugs or promiscuity," explained psychologist Dr Glen Wilson of the University of London.

"People have a psychological need for role models and kids live vicariously through the stars they follow. They dream of being famous like them. Kylie is an approachable star but with glamour that grows as she becomes more famous. It is rather like the older generation's fascination with the Royal Family," he added.

Kylie had no intention of losing this unique hold over her public and was careful to combine her raunchier moments with reminders of her more innocent past. She still giggled girlishly and reverted to the old tomboy type during TV and radio appearances, cleverly signalling to her fans that even if she had become their older sister, she was still their favourite sister.

Her carefully planned, almost militarily precise, campaign again worked. The tour, the endless TV appearances and promotion

catapulted her second album 'Enjoy Yourself' straight to the top of the UK album charts at the end of October 1989. Within three weeks it had sold a staggering 600,000 copies in the UK alone.

When, just as Kylie ended her ten date tour, the UK's top pop magazine *Smash Hits* held its annual awards ceremony, her position as music's No 1 female star was unassailable.

Kylie swept the board as she was voted best female singer and "most fanciable female". *Neighbours*, the show she was about to be seen leaving on British TV screens, was voted top TV show and her co-star Jason Donovan carried off four awards too. It was a day of sweet triumph for Kylie, her long time friend Jason and Stock, Aitken and Waterman, the musical masterminds behind them.

Dressed in a gold sequined bra and spangly pink shorts, Kylie rounded off her visit to the UK with an electric live performance to the 8,000 fans gathered at London's newest pop venue, The London Arena in Docklands. Not even a highly-publicised- and subsequently denied – exchange between her and jealous rival Wendy James of the band Transvision Vamp – Wendy: "I don't know how they could vote for that Aussie Bimbo, she sounds like my dog." Kylie: "What's your problem?" Wendy: "This whole thing is pathetic, that's my problem" – could take the shine off one of the highlights of Kylie's career.

She had come through her sternest test, she had proven the singing budgie brigade was woefully wrong and that she was now ready to take her career into the even more rarified atmosphere occupied by only a tiny handful of superstars. She had overcome the barrier of playing live, and now she was truly unleashed.

MARKETING A SUPERSTAR

Behind the saccharine - sweet smile and ever feminine image, Kylie hides a shrewd and sometimes ruthless business acumen.

And by the end of 1989 the accountant's daughter was at the centre of one of the most efficient management machines the entertainment world has yet seen, merciless marketing wringing seemingly every dollar, Deutschmark, pound and yen out of her global popularity.

So successful had the Minogue Machine become that it was then able to turn down one of the most lucrative deals in pop music history.

The offer came from one of the industry's most powerful promoters, Mel Bush. Bush, whose thirty years in the music business has brought collaborations with virtually every major star – including Mick Jagger, David Bowie, Elton John and Bryan Ferry – believed Kylie's pulling power would have filled London's Wembley Arena for a record ten successive nights. He offered her a massive £1 million fee for what would have been a historic concert series.

"Her camp turned it down," he explained weeks later, still incredulous at the decision.

Bush, whose discoveries in his three decades

have included the likes of A-Ha, did not go lightly into making his offer. Methodically, meticulously, he studied every aspect of Kylie's talent and music before committing himself to what would have been one of the most ambitious projects even he had attempted.

"You can't really compare Kylie with anyone else around at the moment, and probably never will. She is incomparable and in business terms she is perfect. Perfect for campaigning with, perfect for posters, TV, films and interviews,"

"She's no dumb blonde . . . she has got a skin of steel."

said Bush a tall, silver-haired man who speaks in the burr of his native Wiltshire in England's West Country.

"She's no dumb blonde, she has got a skin of steel and by the way she conducts herself you can tell she has got things in proportion too. Her outlook, unlike so many, and remember she is still 21, is tinged with reality," he added.

Bush too was being realistic when he made his move to stage her first live concerts. He began making plans to fill Wembley Arena with 12,000 people a night, convinced there were more than enough Kylie fans waiting to see her. "I think there are enough fans out there to fill the place ten times over," he said.

Bush envisaged a spectacular stage show including a series of showstopping dance routines.

"I am not a gambler, I look at ten year careers not ten minute careers and I believe Kylie has all the potential necessary to have a very long life span in this business," he said.

"She can go on to be a latter day Judy Garland. Kylie can sing, act and dance and is unique."

But despite his confidence in Kylie and his willingness to give her complete control over her shows, Bush was turned down.

"They obviously have their own marketing strategy and who can argue against that. It has worked marvellously well for her so far," he said philosophically.

"But I would like to have seen her perform at bona fide concerts to prove her critics wrong. People always knock someone who has achieved a great deal in a short time. I am sure she would have succeeded," he added.

Bush was not the first senior industry figure to be left dumbstruck by the single-minded approach Kylie and her advisers were taking. Astute team that they were – from Kylie herself, through father Ron and Svengali Blamey to PR people Sally Atkins and the McCright brothers Ron and Rob – they were aware they had been dealt a one-off set of cards. They were determined to play them carefully – and for the biggest jackpot possible.

Kylie resisted Bush's offers of live glory because, as she had felt earlier when PWL had first extended pressure on her to go on tour, it did not fit properly into the strategy mapped out for her. Live work was for the future and would follow when Kylie felt fully ready for the demands of life on the road – and for now there were a million other business opportunities to be pursued.

In the three years since she had broken through as a pop star, Kylie has constructed a network of companies to handle her affairs. The companies, distributed around the world in the nations where her popularity was spreading like wildfire, were run by teams of solicitors and accountants in turn managed by Kylie's supremo, Terry Blamey. Kylie, father Ron, mum Carol and the rest of the family, held the controlling shares in this worldwide empire. The mother company, Kylie Incorporated, remained based in Australia.

The empire's goal was simple – to maximise the income Kylie, her records, videos and massive merchandising could earn. And at the heart of that operation was a crackdown on outsiders the Minogue machine felt were unfairly cashing in on her success.

Like every star before her Kylie was painfully aware that her fame and popularity could wane literally overnight. But few celebrities worked so hard to ensure that the proceeds from the golden years all ended up in her coffers. Kylie believed that her image – the sound, the clothes the carefully constructed "look" that millions around the world copied – belonged exclusively to her.

In America in particular lawyers were accepting protests from stars who claimed their image was "intellectual property" which should only be reproduced with their permission. A New York clothes store was taken to court after using a lookalike of comic Woody Allen while Ford Motor Company was alleged to have duplicated Bette Midler's voice without permission. Kylie determined to be at the forefront of moves to get the same principles introduced in Australia and Britain.

copyright," he added.

By the end of 1989, however, the relentless way in which Kylie's team tracked the "pirates" had turned what had been a tide into something nearer a trickle. "They have basically scared a lot of people," said the head of one top London photographic agency. "Now there are people around who are saying, 'I wish I had never bothered taking a picture of Kylie Minogue'," he added ruefully.

Controlling the way her image was seen around the world ensured that Kylie made the most of her success as her face became familiar all across the globe. But more astute moves made even before she had established herself as a world star had guaranteed that she collected an above average share of the money her records were making.

Kylie signed a unique record deal linking the independent Australian label Mushroom Records with Stock, Aitken and Waterman's PWL. Mushroom had been Kylie's first record company, releasing her début single 'The Locomotion' in Australia in July 1987. When PWL re-recorded the song in Australia the two companies formed a joint venture. The partnership – called PAL Productions – looked

This girl's no dummy . . . Kylie and a lifesize cardboard cutout of herself at the London launch of her debut album, simply titled Kylie. What else?

It was the use of "pirate" photographs of herself which most upset and frustrated Kylie. She claimed photographers who took pictures of her as she walked the streets or appeared at public events were then making a fortune by selling their shots to companies ready to churn out posters, T-shirts and magazines by the million. Whenever she appeared on stage or at TV stations she insisted cameramen signed forms preventing them from selling their pictures to these "pirate" merchandisers. Kylie's organisation believed the unofficial pictures were literally losing their star millions and whenever they saw those pictures on sale they moved to sue the publishers. But they were often frustrated.

"People who cobble together magazines on anyone famous turn it into a sandbag affair," said PWL managing director David Howells in an interview with Australia's Business Review Weekly in January 1989. "They create a poster that turns into a booklet. Whenever we try to stop it, and our lawyers attempt to track down who is behind these publications, they have sold out and disappeared. It happens with the music too. These outside bodies are bootlegging albums, producing unauthorised products and breaching

after all her recording rights wherever her records were released, licensing Kylie's music to major labels in different countries. Linking up with PWL – unique in the way they were songwriters, producers and publishers – meant there was more money to go around.

"The great thing about PAL is the backing of Stock, Aitken and Waterman. Their string of hits means PAL's negotiating position on royalties is much stronger," said Gary Ashley, Mushroom's general manager. The deal also meant that Kylie could be given a better than average contract, he revealed in Business Review Weekly. "Once she

was a hit, we could have sat on the first contract and made more money from her. But that isn't fair. One thing we learned from her success is that there is enough money for all if there is no greed," he added.

"The joint venture means money for all if there is no greed," he added. "We are all doing well but so is Kylie." The article claimed Kylie currently collects $1 for every $17 she earns.

As she became a phenomenon across the world Kylie and her organisation also began looking at sponsorship and allowing the star's image to be associated with High Street products. The fresh-faced, girl-

next-door image could not be allowed to be tarnished by being linked with the wrong merchandise and the negotiations that went into choosing the first Kylie-recommended products were intense. Eventually, however, the breakthrough was made in Japan where a £1 million deal saw the country's favourite singer endorsing cars and electrical goods in TV, poster and newspaper campaigns.

A deal was even signed allowing a telephone company to carry a hologram picture of Kylie on credit cards used in Japan's public phone boxes. In Britain it was the face of William Shakespeare that had been chosen to become the first hologramic image used on credit cards. This was

the status the Mighty Minogue was now enjoying in the Land of the Rising Sun.

As Kylie's business empire was already planning for the 1990s – estimates of its overall earnings are now a staggering £4.5 million a month – virtually every music executive in the world was casting an envious eye at what was being acknowledged as one of the best business operations pop had ever seen.

And at the centre of it was Kylie – the tough cookie refusing to crumble.

"It has been her acting experience, being in front of cameras from an early age which sets her apart. If she was just a pop star she would not be able to do it," said Mel Bush.

"It has given her a head start over everyone else and trained her in the art of being able to look after herself. People make jokes about her but her great strength is her unaffected personality and ability to communicate. These people, like Jagger, Bowie and Ferry have all got something you can feel, but not see; a rare ability to have charismatic contact with people," he added.

"I have seen at first hand her effect on people young and old. Believe me, she was worth a million pound offer . . . "

KYLIE'S GREEN CRUSADE

I f it all came to an end tomorrow, the last person to worry would be Kylie. Sure, her management team would be left without a breadwinner. Her publicists would have to search for other stars to publicise.

But Kylie? She'd go back home to Oz and open a shop, maybe two. More likely a chain.

Since she was a schoolgirl she's dreamed of owning shops. Possibly even more so than being the all singing, all dancing performer which made her a millionairess.

The only difference is that all that acting, all that recording, all that boring, frightening flying to gigs gave her the cash to fulfil that dream. As a teenager she planned to open shops supplying the stuff modern youngsters' dressing tables are weighed down with. "Essential oils," said the young Kylie. "I love them, and I'd love to own shops selling them."

Even in her mass-selling video-tape, *Kylie The Videos*, she tells her fans: "How long will it last? Who knows? "There are still tons of things I want to do and this is the sort of place I'd love to have," says Kylie, walking to one of her favourite shops in her home country.

"Selling things like scented drawer liners. Essential oils, country gardening books . . . all sorts of knicknacks."

But a year after that home-made PWL mini movie, featuring her hits, 'The Locomotion', 'I Should Be So Lucky', 'Got To Be Certain', and 'Je Ne Sais Pas Pourquoi', for her devotees to play in their homes, Kylie was really considering a major career move if everything went wrong. She was planning her crusade to become a Green politician.

If not directly representing the official political party just yet, she was anxious to push her views and get her army of young fans to

"I think Green issues are very, very important."

follow suit, and help save the planet.

According to close friends, Green issues were beginning to take over her life in a very big way.

Towards the end of 1989 film and TV scripts were flooding in at an unprecedented rate, spurred on by her successful début live tour, the incredible success, even by her standards, of her second album 'Enjoy Yourself' which entered the British LP charts at number one on its first day of

The beautiful Yarra River in Melbourne. Kylie's support for the green crusade was formed during her childhood years growing up surrounded by the abundance of natural beauty in her native land.

release in October that year and the much-anticipated release of *The Delinquents*.

TV, advertising and movie moguls around the world wanted a slice of the Kylie action and sent her their offers on paper.

Unfortunately for them, many of the proposed deals and screenplays were printed on ordinary paper. What they did not know was Kylie's principles now prevented her from even touching them. She would only read them if they were Green: written on re-cycled paper.

Kylie was so convinced of the importance of going Green whenever possible, she insisted that the album sleeve for 'Enjoy Yourself' was made out of re-cycled paper.

Her camp confirms the lengths to which Kylie is prepared to go to maintain the environment-friendly campaign and reveals she REFUSES to handle everyday plastics, because they cannot be broken down naturally and pose a threat to the habitat.

Her policy often shocks airline stewardesses because the singer won't touch artificial food containers. It isn't just that she doesn't have the stomach to eat anything because of her morbid dread of flying; more that she can't accept touching anything anti-Green.

The millionairess learned about Green issues, the dangers facing the world and how individuals could help the planet fight back, by endless reading on the subject.

One of the ways she helps the endangered ecosystem is by always throwing her left-over food on the land, and not in the rubbish bin because its nutrients are valuable as organic fertilizer.

Kylie's bible has been Gaia's *Atlas Of Planet Management*. She dragged the heavy tome along with her when she went on tour to Japan to give her plenty of bed time reading on her favourite subject.

Kylie admitted: "I think Green issues are very, very important and everyone should get involved wherever they can and take notice of the problems.

"I do what I can to help and one day I would really like a shop full of Green products. I love shops anyway, so it would make sense to stock products that don't damage the environment."

One of Kylie's entourage, an aide and friend, explained: "She has been studying the Atlas carefully for nearly two months, before she is ready to step on a soap box or address meetings.

She realises that with her influence on millions of youngsters, she can now use her position to do some good."

She plans to encourage her predominantly teenaged followers take an interest in politics at a grass-roots level. She would urge them to either aim to become local councillors and get involved in important decision-making, or lobby the authorities to take more steps to protect the environment by providing more things like facilities for recycling household refuse.

Her friend added: "She also wants to campaign for paper not plastic bags at supermarkets and is angry that the catering industry uses too much plastic in packaging, because it is almost impossible to break down without causing pollution.

She takes the whole subject very seriously and intends to become very involved in Green issues at all kinds of levels in future. It is not that she's a political animal, just someone who has seen a lot of beautiful places in the world; feels very fortunate to be in such a privileged position because of her successful TV and recording career, and so wants to put a bit back into a world which has so far been very kind to her."

Kylie's love of nature is now a huge influence on her life. In fact, her affection for the wonderful world in which she lives has helped her survive. She long ago learned that the pressure of fame and the goldfish bowl existence it brings can take a terrible toll.

The horror of the near nervous breakdown she suffered soon after launching her recording career, as she struggled to combine acting with singing, was taken by her as a warning to calm down.

So Kylie, never one to let a lesson pass unheeded, acted on it. To relieve the strain she turned to painting, a pastime she has loved since childhood.

Kylie has always had an eye for composition and colour, and is particularly gifted in the art of watercolour. So, like Prince Charles and thousands of less well known amateur artists, Kylie now sits at her easel and loses herself in another world. Alone with her thoughts and with a blank canvas in front of her, she is transported far away from the rough and occasionally ruthless showbusiness industry.

Paintbrush in hand, Kylie recalls the beautiful things in life as she creates her own, very individual, landscapes, portraits and still lifes. But sadly the works of art are not destined for any gallery . . . they remain a very private and personal part of Kylie's life.

"She's very creative," says PWL managing director David Howells, one of the few music industry figures who have seen Kylie's work. "She paints beautiful water colours."

"She has always been that way, ever since she was a little girl," says another of those close to her, Kylie's great aunt, Mrs Thomas Riddiford. "She had only to see something once and she remembered it. It was the same with singing. She picks things up very quickly."

Occasionally, however, Kylie does let the world have a glimpse of her talent. When an Australian magazine, *Cleo*, asked a number of celebrities to submit self portraits, Kylie couldn't resist. And when a psychologist analysed her drawing, he cast a fascinating new light on Kylie, the amateur artist.

Kylie's drawing was deliberately childlike. She presented herself as a mass of curly hair, decorated with huge teeth and knobbly knees. Underneath she scrawled the words, "The real me. Love, Kylie."

"We could say Kylie's just having fun, being a big kid, giving us a giggle; but then the grown up Kylie goes and writes a caption to go with the picture," began the psychologist's summing up.

"So she wants us to pay a bit more attention, to think about it a bit. So we think: is she saying that behind the glamour and the adulation, especially from young girls, she is really just one of them? We can go a bit further with the analysis, and look at what sort of young girl she is depicting. Well, the girl in the drawing is, to say the least, not very conventionally sexual, what with the tiny breasts, demure dress, big feet, those knees and rather daffy expression.

"She is, however, saying a lot of things about young feelings: Kylie wanting to love and be loved at the same time.

"Those outstretched arms, that big smile, seem to tell two things," said the psychologist. Concluding his telling analysis, he added: "Firstly there's a Kylie that wants to play like a kid and secondly there's a more subtle Kylie with an appeal. 'Please take notice that I sometimes need to be the real me', is what she seems to be really saying through the way she's portrayed herself."

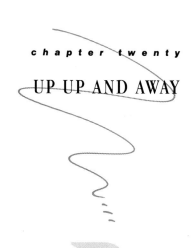

UP UP AND AWAY

By December 1989 Kylie's sugar coated image had melted for good. No matter how hard she protested that *The Delinquents* was not soft porn, the film transformed her into the sex-siren she secretly desired to become.

There were no hard core scenes, but Kylie was talking dirty, kicking off her underwear in bedroom antics and begging co-star Charlie Schlatter's character to make love to her.

And that was only in the trailer for the movie!

The final scene in the original trailer had to be cut because Lola screams passionately: "I love it when he kisses me. I love the way he looks when he's just about to . . ."

Film chiefs thought Kylie uttering such abandoned words were not suitable for a clip to advertise the film at British cinemas under a 'PG' – Parental Guidance – certificate.

The image had been shattered. The virginal singer had, at least, lost her maidenhood on screen – and had loved every pulsating minute of it.

Kylie had come of age and become a sensuous woman, just like Monroe, whom she had always loved being likened to.

But what of those love-making scenes with Schlatter, the hunky 23-year-old New Jersey boy, much experienced in the art of film-making and a man of the world? How had it felt for him?

"They were difficult to do," Charlie admitted. "I have never done a romantic film before. I had never had to do love scenes and neither had Kylie. Technically they are a problem. A lot of people get the wrong idea. You don't just jump between the sheets and say, 'Hey, let's go for it. Let's have a free for all'.

"The love scenes are all finely choreographed ballets. I don't think anyone will find them offensive. If they do then I'm sorry, but there is nothing vile or nasty about what we did.

"It is a romantic movie about two young people very much in love and all that goes with that. I think anyone who has been in love will like this movie. It isn't just for kids. People who are in their 40s and 50s will like it also, because this is about two kids from their generation. I play a guy who finds love and then people try to take it away. It is very moving."

But how did Charlie feel kissing and making love to one of the pop world's latest idols, especially as some on-set mischief makers suggested the two had got on *so* well, their celluloid games carried on into real life.

Charlie, who didn't have a girlfriend at the time, hit back: "I am an actor and doing scenes like that is what I am paid to do. So of course we got emotional, and if it looks real then that is great, that is the way it should be.

"I enjoyed Kylie's company a lot. I think she is great, a nice person and a fine actress and we developed a great working relationship.

"I hadn't heard about her or her music before we met. I have listened to a few of her tracks since and I like them. She is a very talented singer too. I hope to see her again soon.

I will be going to Australia for a holiday and I hope we can meet up, if work allows, because she is very busy, just like me.

"Like I said, I enjoyed being with her, but you would have to be some kind of retard to get turned on in those scenes by thinking I am kissing a sex symbol . . . I mean I was just doing my job. You don't think about anything else apart from getting it right in front of the cameras."

When they first met, Charlie called the shots by improvising in front of the cameras and using his experience from films like *Bright Lights, Big City*, with Michael J Fox, and *18 Again*, with George Burns.

He said: "Kylie was a little nervous when I improvised and it threw her off. But she got used to me and started to do it herself and in the end we were both very comfortable and relaxed."

He was aware of the controversial scene which had to be cut from the trailer and laughed at the problems it caused in the UK.

"I have yet to see a trailer that is anything reminiscent of the film it promotes," he said. "The distributors have their job to do in getting people into theatres to watch their movie. It is up to them and a lot of the time they will do anything to get you inside. I know the line you are talking about, but she never says the final word, although it is pretty obvious what she means.

"But I think it is acceptable. it is about two people in love after all."

As a new decade dawns, Kylie Minogue's place as one of the all-round entertainers of her generation is secure. Just turned 21, she has sold more than 30 million records worldwide, has made a major feature film and has silenced the carping critics with a massively successful début tour as a live performer. Along the way she has also matured into a beautiful young woman.

Hollywood already has her marked as one of the hottest properties of the 1990s, a shining star equipped to inherit the mantle of Marilyn Monroe.

Kylie however has her sights set on another star, and another decade, the 1940s. Until she paid the ultimate price of fame, Judy Garland was the most gifted star of them all. She blossomed from a precocious teenager in films like *The Wizard Of Oz* into a charismatically attractive woman with towering talent, able to sing, dance and act like no one before or since.

As her first movie *The Delinquents* – aided by some pre-release hype over Australian clerics calling for sexy scenes between her and handsome co-star Charlie Schlatter to be cut – opened around the world at the end of 1989, Kylie was planning a move that could set her on that same yellow brick road to showbusiness immortality.

Her dream is to make a movie musical, a multi-million celluloid spectacle, in which she can prove to the world that her three year apprenticeship is over. Like every other step she has taken, this – her most ambitious yet – is being planned with painstaking attention to detail. And she has entrusted the musical Midases who have turned all she has touched so far to gold with the job of making her a new Garland.

Stock, Aitken and Waterman will write the music for the spectacular, which will get under way early in the new decade. The world must wait however to discover whether Kylie will be cast as some lovelorn, tragic Juliet to Jason's Romeo or whether her musical will, in the mould of *The Delinquents*, be a rock and roll high

Kylie's idols. The hit movie Grease, starring John Travolta and Olivia Newton-John, is one of Kylie's all time favourites.

school blockbuster, like *Grease*, the movie she admits she has loved since her Melbourne childhood.

PWL are keeping their plans a closely guarded secret. "Yes, there are plans for a musical, it is true we are talking about doing one with Kylie and we all very much want it to happen," admitted Pete Waterman. "But at the moment nothing has been firmed up. We will write the songs as soon as we can sort out our other commitments. It is obviously a very exciting project for us though, and it will allow Kylie to show just how much she has developed over the past three years.

"It still amazes me how much she has come on and is improving all the time. A musical is a natural vehicle for her to pull all her talents together," he added.

Such is Kylie's potential in the eyes of the showbusiness speculators of Hollywood however that the musical may have to wait until she has made another movie. The lure of Tinseltown and the magic dollar was always going to prove irresistible to someone as unashamedly ambitious as Kylie, and so it is proving.

"I will probably do a film in America next year," she confirmed late in 1989. "I would really like to do a comedy."

And she confirmed the inevitable, the news that executives back at Grundy TV in Melbourne had always feared they would hear, she would never again play Charlene in *Neighbours*.

"When I left it was open ended so that if things did not work out for me I could go back to playing Charlene. Now though it is all very secure for me so I will not be going back," she said. "I was there for two and a half years, now I would just like to keep my happy memories."

Those 'happy memories' were soured, however, in Victoria's Supreme Court on November 16, 1989. It was then that Kylie and Terry Blamey – now experienced legal hands – suffered a rare courtroom setback. Australian Supreme Court Judge Barry Beach kicked out their attempt to stop Grundy Television from releasing a special *Neighbours* video based on Kylie's screen romance with Jason.

Neighbours: The Scott And Charlene Love Story, in which Kylie would once more be seen in oilstained overalls as the tomboy mechanic from Ramsay Street, would damage her new sophisticated image, they claimed. Judge Beach disagreed and refused to grant an injunction.

He ruled that Kylie, who had refused permission for the video when approached by

Grundy, had a weak case because she owed much of her success to *Neighbours*. And he said that the video was 'just a drop in the bucket of *Neighbours* memorabilia'.

The decision left Kylie 'hurt and angry' said Blamey after the ruling. She was distressed at the 'ill treatment and disrespect' Grundy had shown her, he added. Kylie was also far from happy that she wasn't benefiting from the video. "She's not getting paid one cent as far as we know. She feels used," said Blamey.

The episode left Kylie and Grundy enemies. "She was a nobody when she first came to us and now she's trying to bite the hand that fed her," said a spokesman for the TV company bitterly.

But both sides knew it finally confirmed what they already knew. There was now more chance of hiring Marlon Brando for a cameo on *Neighbours* than getting Kylie back.

Strange as the taste of defeat was, however, Kylie shrugged off the episode and instead carried on looking to the future. She was consoled in the knowledge that no-one would believe a girl next door like her any more anyway.

A multi-millionairess with a fortune estimated

at more than £10 million, a property tycoon in Australia where she was spending a fortune renovating her latest acquisition, a mammoth Victorian town house in the Melbourne suburbs, a singer poised to come of age with a backing band of her own and a world tour – the hologramic face of high technology in Japan, how could she ever again have been expected to have slipped into oily dungarees to tinker with the engine of a Land Rover?

Already wise to the ways of two of the most notoriously sharkish industries, TV and pop, Kylie was not however going to Hollywood with her eyes closed. The shrewd little girl from Australia had no intention of following others who had been eaten by the star system and dumped at the end of it all with nothing.

Hard bargains were being driven before she agreed to make her Hollywood début and she was already planning to take control by producing – and maybe directing – her own movies. Staying in control had always been Kylie's top priority, not even the most powerful entertainment men in the world were going to interfere with that.

"I'm planning to direct and produce my own films eventually," she revealed.

The girl who used to cry at criticism was now fireproof. Nothing could dent the self belief that was driving her on to new heights.

She summed it all up like this: "People try to put you down and say, 'You are just manufactured. You're a puppet'. If I was a manufactured product I wouldn't still be here. I wouldn't be able to sit in this room talking without someone's hand up my back, moving my mouth for me."

The Queen of Pop stayed aloof on her throne, as the arguments about her ability continued to rage around her.

Waterman and infamous 70's starmaker Jonathan King rowed publicly over her.

King, reviled by many, but acknowledged as an expert in the cynical exploitation of the pop world sniped: "I thought when Kylie Minogue did 'I Should Be So Lucky, Lucky, Lucky,' it was one of the most awful things I have ever heard. This was a totally untalented Australian soap actress. I have no interest in her whatsoever."

But on closer examination he was forced to admit even he may have been wrong, and he demanded that the PWL stable looked after its young charges Kylie and Jason and prevented them from destroying their lives.

He said: "Some of the Kylie Minogue records are actually very cleverly constructed, well put together. When you listen to one of the rather better Kylie records, they have taken a girl who doesn't really have a great voice, who is an actress, and slowly they have developed a career where she actually now has a sound which is similar to some of the girly groups in the 60's, in a totally different way.

"A lot of people would never deny the Shangri-Las, a great band produced by Shadow Morton, were fake girl singers going along with the producer's ideas."

He was worried about Kylie's future welfare and insisted that Waterman and Co explained the problems she, and Jason for that matter, would face when it all ended.

He warned: "It is easy to be has-beens at 21 with nothing in the future and for their lives to be ruined.

"I know it sounds bizarre to say that when someone has made an awful lot of money and had a lot of fame and adulation, but you can wreck their minds, you can wreck their self-ego and esteem by giving them the whole wrong picture of themselves by pretending they are good at one thing when they are not and boosting other things.

"A good manager and record company has to explain this will go so far and stop."

Waterman hit back saying both Kylie and Jason knew they were successful actors before their pop success and were aware of the dangers.

PWL's managing director David Howells entered the debate on Kylie's future by insisting she had the qualities to see her endure in the same way pop's Peter Pan Cliff Richard had.

"I heard Kylie sing and I was 17 again, and raving about Cliff," said Howells, now 48.

"To me she was, and is, blessed with that wonderful thing that got me so excited about Cliff all those years ago – a unique voice. I recognised it right away, and I was on Cloud Nine. What she has to offer is precisely what has seen Cliff through 31 years of showbusiness.

"I saw a headline on an article about Kylie once which read 'I should be so ordinary' and I thought, 'Yeah, that's exactly right'. That's what she is. It's a great compliment to her.

"She's such a success she appeals to people who like her. She does it a little better than most, that's all.

"She paints the most beautiful watercolours, she sews, she knits, she makes a lot of her own clothes even though she could probably afford the entire shop which sells them. She's very creative.

"She doesn't look upon herself as a special person, a fairytale creature in an ivory tower.

She's far too sensible for that.

"The hard part is not letting it go to your head, but I can't see Kylie making that mistake. As long as she approaches everything with as much fascination and energy as she does now, she'll retain her freshness forever.

"Kylie is smart. She was aware of that from the beginning without being told or taught. She has always known that it's the fans who count."

Howells maintained that Kylie represented the UP side of life and would be a continuing pop power because she would never lose the sense of fun she injected into every new project.

"Fans have been growing bored with the sex and drugs and rock and roll syndrome. Youth and innocence are back in. Kylie's audience relates to her perfectly. She's still full of the joys of spring. If she can retain the mood, she's laughing," said Howells.

He admitted his hit factory had stagemanaged much of her career, using the age-old ploy of staying ahead of the game.

"A lot of it is instinct, though," he admitted. "You either have it or you don't.

"Kylie is changing all the time, she has never let a trend take hold of her. However she dresses herself, that's what she becomes. She slips on a bright red party dress and she becomes a fun teenager. Or she zips herself into a black evening gown and she's a sophisticated 30 year old.

"Kylie is not afraid to explore all styles. You can never describe her as having a particular image. In fact, no one can keep up with her.

"As long as she can maintain the ability to keep moving forward that fast and stay ahead of the game, she is winning."

Another tribute came from an independent source, and a man who knows what he is talking about.

Lyricist Tim Rice, one of the forces behind worldwide musical smashes *Chess*, *Jesus Christ Superstar* and *Evita*, summed up: "You can't fool hundreds of thousands, or millions of people at the same time with absolute garbage for record after record.

"I think if Kylie Minogue has been a flash in the pan she would have lasted for a couple of singles. It looks like she's going to last for a lot more than that."

Kylie will never forget the major role PWL played in changing her life, making a millionairess out of a minor TV star, and is prepared to defend them to the hilt.

"They get an awful lot of criticism, simply because they are successful," she said. "They are not magic. They don't just touch something and it just works. They are where they are because they are experienced, professional and talented.

"The pressure that they are under to keep coming up with hit songs . . . for people trying to write just one, that can be difficult. So I really respect and admire them.

"If that is what they are good at doing and I'm good at singing and projecting my image, that's what we should stick to, and that's why we are having so much success."

So after two bewildering years, millions of pounds both banked and still rolling in, Kylie expects to live off her celebrity status well into the 21st Century.

And it is Britain she thanks for the startling transformation and thinks will keep her at the top.

"If you are a star there, you're a star forever," she said.